THE OLDEST GOD

THE OLDEST GOD

THE OLDEST

Archaic Religion Yesterday & Today

Denise Lardner Carmody

ABINGDON / NASHVILLE

THE OLDEST GOD

Copyright © 1981 by Abingdon

Library of Congress Cataloging in Publication Data

CARMODY, DENISE LARDNER, 1935-
   The Oldest God.
   Includes bibliographies and index.
   1. Religion, Primitive. 2. Religions. I. Title
BL430.C37   291   80-25499

ISBN 0-687-28813-4

Manufactured by the Parthenon Press at
Nashville, Tennessee, United States of America

For

Virgina and Thérèse

Preface

This book is an introductory look at archaic religion, hence its wide scope and synthetic intent. For first-level courses in religious studies, or laypersons' first orientation to this subject matter, comprehensiveness and a synthetic focus seemed imperative. The readings listed at the end of each chapter supply the next level of complexity, though even there I have limited myself to English sources, since most of the readers I envision will find foreign-language work impractical.

I have received help from several sources and would like to acknowledge them here. The Office of Research and Sponsored Programs of Wichita State University supplied financial support. My husband, John Carmody, provided a writer's counsel on many points. Karla Kraft of Wichita State University typed the manuscript expertly. To all of them my sincere thanks.

Denise Lardner Carmody

Contents

Introduction 11
The Meaning of Archaic Religion 11
Matter and Form in This Book 16
Bibliography 20

PART 1: Archaic Religion Yesterday 21

Chapter 1: Prehistoric Religion 22
Paleolithic Hunters and Shamans 22
Neolithic Farmers and the Goddess 31
The Megalith Builders 41
The Wonder of Metal 46
Summary: The Prehistoric Religious Mind 50
Bibliography 52

Chapter 2: Civilizational Religion 54
The Rise of Civilization 54
Egypt 59
Greece 68
The Cosmological Myth 72
Bibliography 75

Chapter 3: Archaism in the World Religions 76
Buddhism 77
Christianity 83
Islam 90
Summary:Archaism in the World Religions 95
Bibliography 97

PART II: Archaic Religion Today 99

Chapter 4: American Indian Religion 100
Diversity and Unity 100
American Indian Rituals 105
American Indian Ecology 114
Case Study: The American Indian Child 119
Bibliography 123

Chapter 5: African Religion 125
Major Concepts of God 125
Sacrifice and Rites of Passage 131
Religious Authority Figures 137
Case Study: An Aged Contemporary Pygmy 144
Bibliography 149

Chapter 6: Australian Religion 150
The Australian Mythic World 150
The Australian Medicine Man 156
Case Study: Sacrality in the Feminine Life-Cycle 162
Indians, Africans, Australians: Common Themes 168
Bibliography 173

Conclusion 175
Modernity and the Archaic 175
The Oldest God 180
Bibliography 184

Index 185

Introduction

The Meaning of Archaic Religion

Archaic religion is concrete, close to bodily life. Let us therefore start to study it concretely, through stories drawn from three archaic peoples.

An Anglo graduate student, adopted by an elderly Navaho man as his "son," was attempting to prepare his "father" for a visit to a large city. It was to be the old Navaho's first contact with white culture on a large scale. The son showed the father a large photo of the Empire State Building. "How many sheep will it hold?" the old man asked. Puzzled, the son explained that the building held people, not sheep. That in turn puzzled the father: People would pack themselves into a vertical tomb like that? How would they breathe? How would they relieve themselves? When the son explained air-conditioning and toilets, the father was horrified. Artificial air, special rooms for human waste—no wonder whites are so crazy. They live in a polluted atmosphere, and so they must have polluted spirits.

The picture of the Empire State Building showed a plane overhead. The old man had seen small planes flying over the reservation, and they had made him vaguely uneasy. When the son described the huge size of a modern bomber, the father again asked, "How many sheep will it hold?" This time the son realized what he meant: What "use" does this thing have, in terms of my experience? For instance, how does it translate into terms of sheep herding? The son therefore explained that bombers basically function to hold explosives and drop them on one's enemy. This horrified the old man far more than the Empire State Building had. To kill hundreds of human beings from so far off that you could barely see them—that was just barbarous. No thank you—there would be no trip to the city. Culture like the white man's was best kept far away. (See Toelken.)*

In this small clash between the archaic culture of an American Indian and the current culture of an industrialized white, one has a first glimpse of several profound differences. For the old Navaho, the natural environment was crucially important. He did not distinguish between humans, animals, plants, and minerals the way people of New York do. Rather, everything in his world was a fellow-citizen, a fairly equal participant in a living space shared democratically. The quality of that living space—its air, openness, quiet—affected intimately the human beings who dwelt within it. So did the quality of the relations between human beings and animals, human beings and plants. To breathe artificial air was to risk an artificial soul. To block oneself from the sun was to grow cold in spirit, for the world was an organic whole, a continuum of creatures meant to be brotherly and sisterly. It was one sacred totality, not a patchwork of things holy and things profane. Thus in the spring Pueblo Indians would remove the heels from their shoes, because Mother Earth was pregnant. When an Anglo observer asked a Pueblo whether he really believed this would help the crops, the Pueblo replied, "Well, I really don't know whether removing my heels makes a difference or not, but your unwillingness to remove yours certainly shows what kind of person you are."

For most archaic peoples, we moderns are the kind of persons who have lost contact with primary physical realities. Mother Earth is no longer a treasure; we no longer honor the

* Sources cited will be found in the bibliography at the end of the chapter.

source of life. That is why we can ravage the land, pollute the oceans and air, drop down death from miles above. By contrast, close connection to physical nature and absorption with the mystery of life are primary values in archaic religion. They work in our second story, which comes from Africa.

A group of women, chanting loudly, crowd around the prostrate figure of a naked girl. They are present to enact the girl's entrance into full womanhood. At the sign of her first menstruation, the girl was taken outside the tribal village and segregated from her family and friends. Older women instructed her in feminine lore, to prepare her for the responsibilities she would soon assume as a wife and mother. Now the initiation reaches its climax. Her body brightly painted and decorated with grasses, the girl steels herself for the last act. As the chanting reaches fever pitch an old woman kneels between her open legs. Raising a knife high, she plunges it into the girl's genitals and excises the clitoris. The girl bites down hard on the clump of rawhide in her mouth to stifle her screams. She nearly blacks out from the pain, but as her blood flows the singing turns joyous and revives her. She is now a woman, a pure bearer of life. (See MacCormack.)

Clitoridectomy—and other forms of genital mutilation—is widespread. It occurs in parts of Africa, Australia, Central America, South America, and the Arab Middle East. Historically we know from female mummies that it occurred in ancient Egypt. Interpretations of clitoridectomy vary, and current feminists view it darkly (see Daly, pp. 153-77), but no simple read-out is wholly satisfactory. Very likely there have been savage patriarchal causes, and many of the peoples' own explanations carry a grim view of female sexuality. But, in the concrete, archaic women have also affirmed clitoridectomy as a rite of passage—an entry into female adulthood worth its pain because it enhanced their roles as wives and mothers. For instance, the explanation that the clitoris is a penis-like organ, whose removal makes women more womanly, has both rationalized a loss of female pleasure and solidified women's polar opposition to men. The explanation that this painful trial, like the trials that boys undergo (circumcision, loss of fingers, etc.), prepares the initiant for adult endurance is similarly ambivalent. Its focus on women's sex is negative, but its view of adulthood can be quite positive.

To put the best face on it, the African use of clitoridectomy is a way of trying to control the sacral fertility that woman bears. For most archaic peoples, the sacred is a power that can destroy as well as elevate. Therefore most archaic peoples kept menstruating women away from the rest of the tribe. They especially had to stay away from warriors, for the conflict between women's life-power and warriors' killing-power might be explosive. On the other hand, the sacral fertility that came to a woman in her first menstruation stimulated some tribes to unalloyed joy. The Pygmies of Zaire, for instance, celebrated the *elima* when a girl reached adulthood. It was a time of dancing, feasting, and affirmation that their life in the forest was very good. There was no clitoridectomy, and no dark view of women's sex. So too with American Indians such as the Apaches and Sioux. Though they saw dangers in woman-power, they affirmed more profoundly its holy ties to life. Thus the Sioux had a special ceremony for a girl's coming of age, and the Apache thought that Changing Woman, a chief deity, took over the young initiate's body, giving it the blessings of physical strength, an even temperament, and prosperity in old age. The tie of sexuality with life therefore made puberty a key moment in the archaic cycle. In almost all archaic societies, ceremonializing the young adult to harmony with the cosmic powers was a prime concern.

Our third story comes from South America. Along the border of Brazil and Venezuela, a woman of the Yanomamo tribe snatches her bawling little boy from a jungle clearing, where he has just crawled into an army of stinging ants. Alternately crooning and scolding, she tries to hush his wails,

14

for she believes that his soul can escape on a big exhalation. The souls of little ones are mobile; they have not yet anchored themselves in their new locales. Moreover, the witch doctor of an enemy tribe can concentrate his black magic on children, causing a soul-loss that produces sickness or death. Should the woman's baby become sick after being stung, the tribe will call its own witch doctor into action. He will try to lure the soul back to the child's body by gently sweeping the area where the stinging occurred. The soul is very likely lingering there, and if the tribe is fortunate he can lure it back with promises of good times and rewards.

The Yanomamo exemplify the tendency of many archaic peoples to populate the world with spirits. All sorts of fortune, both good and bad, derive from spirits. The good fortune of a successful hunt derives from benign spirits of the jungle, whom an archaic tribe will thank carefully. The bad fortune of sickness or drought derives from malign spirits, whom the tribe will have its witch doctor or shaman try to ward off. In the warlore of the Yanomamo, the shaman takes hallucinogenic snuff to summon tiny humanoid spirits, called *hekura,* who can fight in his people's behalf. (Chagnon, p. 24)

What modern Western cultures deal with scientifically or psychologically, archaic peoples tend to deal with by trying to influence spirits. Navaho sand paintings are a vivid testimony to the healing power archaic people have found in readjusting the spirit to its environment. Rituals of many other archaic peoples depend on a similar assumption: spiritual forces can have decisive physical effects.

Harmony with nature, concern for fertility, interpretation of many events in terms of spiritual forces—these are hallmarks of an *archaic* world-view. We give such concerns this name, without prejudice to their wisdom or foolishness, because they go back to humanity's earliest times. All indications of prehistoric culture lead us to infer that the concern with animals, fertility, and spirits that we observe in nonliterate, small-scale societies of recent times goes back to

THE OLDEST GOD

our very beginnings. The same could be said for most of the
other themes the next pages will document. A tendency to
explain the world by telling a story, a tendency to make such
explanations real by ritualistic ceremony or dance, a tendency
to imagine the world's ultimate powers in terms of fertility
forces—these are suggested by the oldest cave paintings.
Archaic religion therefore is a dealing with the human
situation mythically and organically that is a base-motif in our
species' composition. It produces androgynous (male-female)
gods, rich symbolisms, confusions of imagination and
judgment, and a great stress on spiritual power and harmony.
Our task is to make such a preliminary generalization more
historical and subtle, so that by the end we have caught sight of
the wonderful complexity that archaic religion has evolved.

Matter and Form in This Book

This book is divided into two main parts. Roughly, we are
dealing with archaic religion "yesterday" and "today." Part I,
dealing with yesterday, takes us back to prehistoric beginnings. Such research presents great problems, but archaeologists and prehistorians have slowly accumulated considerable
data on the cultures of Paleolithic hunters.

The first chapter deals with the shamanic world-view of
early hunting cultures and the changes that developments
such as neolithic agriculture brought. For instance, agriculture caused a more sedentary life-style. It gave greater
prominence to women, who probably did most of the earliest
farming, and its religious focus was usually a Great Goddess,
who magnified fertility and sex.

An intriguing portion of the prehistoric story, still not fully
grasped, is the ancestor-veneration and death-cults of the
megalithic (great-stone) cultures, such as that which produced
Stonehenge. At the least, these customs say that the antithesis
of living flesh (the hardest stone) could become a symbol of
the strongest life—of immortality.

The last topic in the first chapter flows from the technology of the Iron Age. Working with iron and fire, miners and smiths changed some of the relations to Mother Earth that agriculturalists enjoyed. By the time of the Iron Age, however, we are on the verge of writing, and so of history proper. Chapter 1 therefore concludes with a summary of the religious "mind" that the longest stretch of human experience, the millennia of prehistoric time, bequeathed to its historical successors.

The second chapter focuses on "civilizational religion." By this we mean the more complex cultural attitudes that followed on the rise of towns and then cities. With a more sedentary and secure life, because of agriculture, and with technological momentum, because of such arts as metal working, the religious conceptions of human beings began to reflect a more adventurous and wide-ranging spirit. At Sumer the discovery of writing and the achievement of a critical cultural-mass produced a burst of creative energy. Often historians of Sumerian civilization disseminate the facts of this cultural process without much interest in its archaic religious roots. By contrast, our concern will be to link Sumerian history with the archaic themes we have developed, showing how such concerns as harmony with nature, fertility, and the influence of spirits assumed new forms.

Chapter 2 also deals with the grander civilizations of Egypt and Greece. Egyptian kingship centered on a profound concern for harmony, and the Egyptian gods Osiris and Re can serve as entry-points to a religious world that stretched from the under-earth (the realm of death) to the heavenly abode of the life-giving sun. Beneath the rich religious mythology of classical Greece lie archaic roots such as the goddess religion of Minoan-Mycenaean times, while parallel to Osiris and Re are the Greek gods Dionysius and Apollo.

Finally, chapter 2 concludes with a discussion of the "cosmological myth," a concept borrowed from Eric Voegelin to generalize about the way civilizational cultures continued to set human affairs within the rhythms of the natural cosmos.

Although scholars debate the extent to which the world religions—those that spread out to inspire several geographically distinct cultures—transcended the cosmological myth, it is clear that some of those religions' higher speculations approached transcendence. Nonetheless, the world-view of the common masses retained many archaic features, and even the founders remained significantly premodern. Chapter 3 therefore focuses on the carry-over of archaic elements in three widely distributed world religions: Buddhism, Christianity, and Islam. In all three we look at ancient aspects of the original message and then at the way the "little tradition," the popular mentality of the peasant classes, remained deeply archaic. Archaism was not the whole story, but it is illuminating to consider Buddha's shamanic and yogic features, Jesus' demonology, and Muhammad's ecstatic visions. Similarly, it is illuminating to consider the spirits that populated folk Buddhism, the witchcraft that warped late-medieval Christianity, and the possessions that bestirred much of popular Islam. As these and other archaic remnants show, the world religions are far from discontinuous with their prehistoric or early civilizational predecessors and are by no means purely "higher" forms that left all archaic traces behind.

Part II deals with archaic religion today—in nonliterate, smaller-scale societies of recent times. From anthropology and the history of religions, we can glean a fair understanding of how American Indians, Africans, and Australians have rung changes on the archaic religious mind into the twentieth century. For example, though the many different Amerindian cultures show considerable diversity, responsible scholars still speak of a significant commonality replete with archaic themes. Chapter 4 will concentrate on ceremonies of the Amerindian life-cycle and what might be called ecological attitudes toward nature. Chapter 5 discusses African religion, stressing the archaism in many tribes' view of divinity, the significance of African sacrifices and rites of passage, and the import of major religious figures (diviners, prophets, kings, etc.). Chapter 6, whose focus is Australia, introduces a wonderful mythology of creation based on eternal ancestors who remain powerful at designated places throughout the land. It also presents the Australian medicine man, a good example of archaic shaminism, and puberty rites that are links to both America and Africa. Chapter 6 concludes by explicating these links so as to synthesize a final impression of archaic religion today.

In the Conclusion I hope to vindicate the form in which I have cast these matters. My idea has been to marry historical studies with contemporary anthropological ones so as to give yesterday and today equal weight (something they usually do not receive). Further, the selected "case studies" in Part II will show how an Indian child, an African elder, and an Australian woman might have experienced an archaic religious world. The Conclusion will draw the different kinds of studies and cases into a sort of tally-sheet—a profit and loss statement on both archaism and modernity. By contrast with archaic peoples, we moderns have both gained and lost some things. One of our gains, though, has been the ability to step outside the world-view we have inherited and recognize some of its deficiencies. By using this ability, we can suggest the place archaic insights might have even tomorrow.

Bibliography

Brown, Joseph Epes, ed. *The Sacred Pipe: Black Elk's Account of the Seven Rites of the Oglala Sioux.* Baltimore, Penguin, 1971.

Chagnon, Napoleon A. *Yanomamo: The Fierce People.* New York: Holt, Rinehart, Winston, 1968.

Collins, John J. *Primitive Religion.* Totowa: Littlefield, Adams & Co., 1978.

Comstock, W. Richard. *The Study of Religion and Primitive Religions.* New York: Harper & Row, 1971.

Daly, Mary. *Gyn/Ecology.* Boston: Beacon Press, 1978.

THE OLDEST GOD

Eiade, Mircea. *Myths, Dreams and Mysteries.* New York: Harper
Torchbooks, 1967.

James, E. O. "Prehistoric Religion." edited by C. Jouco Bleeker and George
Widengren, in *Historia Religionum, I: Religions of the Past,* Leiden: E. J.
Brill, 1969, pp. 23-39.

Jensen, Adolf E. *Myth and Cult Among Primitive Peoples.* Chicago: The
University of Chicago Press, 1963.

MacCormack, Carol P. "Biological Events and Cultural Control." *Signs,* 3/1
(Autumn 1977), 93-100.

Toelken, Barre. "Seeing with a Native Eye: How Many Sheep Will It Hold?"
in *Seeing with a Native Eye,* edited by Walter Holden Capps, New York:
Harper Forum Books, 1976, pp. 9-24.

Turnbull, Colin. *The Forest People: A Study of the Pygmies of the Congo.*
New York: Simon & Schuster, 1962.

Underhill, Ruth M. *Red Man's Religion.* Chicago: The University of Chicago
Press, 1965.

PART I
Archaic Religion Yesterday

Part I deals with archaic peoples of the distant past, who have largely faded from the world's stage. To these peoples, our religious forebears, we owe much in the traditions we have received. From prehistoric times they have kept the world alive with religious significance. Their stories, then, are the first chapters with which any investigation of the oldest God must begin.

Chapter 1:
Prehistoric Religion

Paleolithic Hunters and Shamans

The first true human beings probably lived before 600,000 B.C.E.—how long before, we do not yet know. We do know that around this time fire was being put to domestic uses in the Choukoutien caves of China. The ancestors of these (clearly human) beings who domesticated fire may go back as far as two million years, if present evidences from Africa prove valid. At that distance, however, they are largely shadows in a great darkness.

By the time we have sufficient light to discern prehistoric humans, they have beyond doubt created a culture: that is, they live a group life and are able to pass on skills and beliefs that they develop. Some theoreticians lay great stress on *Homo sapiens'* earlier assumption of an upright posture (on the debt *Homo sapiens* owes *Homo erectus*), for by orienting themselves by reference to their own erect bodies, the earliest humans established an organizing pattern for the division of land, their dwellings, and so forth. Erect, early men and women stood out from the surrounding reality and could organize it anthropocentrically. (See Eliade, 1978a, p. 3.)

From the outset human culture expressed intelligence, imagination, and religion (concern for ultimate meaning). To develop tools, tame fire, use language, and organize cooperative actions, the earliest humans had to be more like than unlike ourselves. A first concern, of course, was securing food. Paleolithic peoples met this concern by hunting and gathering. Hunting made them nomadic: they had to follow the wandering game. Over the millennia, as the earth's temperature varied, human tribes made sizable migrations to the north and south of the Old World. Depending on the prevailing weather, the hunters would camp outside or huddle together inside caves. When they were not actively engaged in the hunt, they would make tools—weapons, knives, needles, rawhide strips. Sharing such tasks, as well as actually hunting and gathering nuts or berries, stimulated communication skills. Paleolithic art suggests that in their spare moments early humans turned such skills to a search for deeper meaning.

Archaic religion roots in this search, as does our own religion today. From paleolithic artifacts, such as carvings on bones, paintings on cave walls, and rough sculptures in stone, we conjecture that paleolithic peoples tried to imagine generalized forces behind the foci of their daily lives. For instance, they tried to imagine a source for the animals they hunted or the berries they ate. Then, attempting sympathetic magic (vivid mimicry thought to induce favorable results), they acted out the good hunt they hoped to have or the fruitful foraging they planned, petitioning the source to be helpful. From both dreams of the day and dreams of the night, they sensed parts of themselves not limited to the here-and-now. Mixing all this together, they focused their search for meaning on the mysterious, crucially important cycles of life and death. In that way sex, birth, hunting, death, and burial became their primary foci. Fertility was a great force, whether in animals, plants, or humans. So too were death and its cognate, the power to kill. Obviously we conjecture about these things, but with a certain probability. For we have enough remains from early burial sites to guide a partial reconstruction of the paleolithic religious mentality.

Treatment of the Dead

In part by using "ethnological parallels" (similarities with recent archaic peoples who are conjectured to be at a similar cultural stage), prehistorians have reached tentative conclusions about some paleolithic practices that illumine the archaic view of death and burial. For example, they think it likely that early nomadic hunters carried with them the skulls of departed loved ones. If so, several inferences are possible. One is that the dead person somehow remained present with the living. Another is that the skull, standing for the brain, represented the seat or organ of life. (Supporting this view are evidences that skulls were put to cultic use—mounted and venerated, probably in hope of securing some help or blessing.) (See Maringer, pp. 18-21.)

From about 50,000 B.C.E., burying the dead was a common practice. With burial, belief in an afterlife apparently became pronounced—at least, an afterlife seems the best explanation for burying the dead with food, utensils, and jewelry; for placing them in a sleeping posture; for rouging them with ochre. That the dead frequently stayed "at home," by being placed under the floor of a cave where people continued to live, suggests that they continued to be members of the family. Another practice, whose meaning is not completely clear, was to bury the dead near the hearth-fire, perhaps so that they might continue to enjoy its warmth. We know from the tenacity of ancestor veneration in East Asia that the dead have long held a profound importance for traditional peoples. But whereas in East Asia recent attitudes toward ancestors have included considerable fear, the domestic aura of the paleolithic practices suggests little fear. On the other hand, there are such early finds as remains of skeletons buried face down or tied like captives, and also what appear to be remains of votive food offerings. Still, a predominance of fear over good feelings probably would have led to burying the dead outside the group's present living quarters. Therefore paleolithic peoples probably did not fear ancestral ghosts greatly.

Other aspects of early burial practices still await full explanation. Why, for instance, should a child have been buried with the shoulder blade of a woolly mammoth? Was this animal so impressive to ice-age peoples that it functioned as a protective deity? Similarly, does burying the deceased in a fetal position indicate that death was conceived as a return to the womb (so as to prelude to rebirth)? Does burial facing east indicate a correlation between the sun and a land of afterlife? And what is the meaning of edging grave sites with animal skulls or of making them places of feasting? These questions, and many more, still await answers. We have found skulls fashioned into cups over an area from northern Spain to Moravia, and the custom of drinking from skull-cups (frequently made from the remains of one's ancestors) is documented in medieval Europe, thirteenth-century Tibet, and nineteenth-century Australia. Does this suggest a strong association between skulls, ancestors, and commemorative celebrations? And what about the use of molars or bits of jaw as decorative pendants? Here too the answers are not certain, for all artifacts ultimately refer to a motivation or intentionality we cannot know. The great likelihood, however, is that paleolithic peoples believed in some kind of continued existence after death and used bone, the most lasting part of physical humanity, to symbolize it.

Hunting and Domestic Rituals

For more than fifty years, scholars have heatedly debated the meaning of evidences that paleolithic bear hunters over a wide area shared a common cultic ritual. The major evidences are bones (skulls and long bones of cave bears) that seem to have been enshrined in wall niches or stone chests in the caves of Switzerland, Germany, France, Yugoslavia, and Austria. One theory suggests that the bears were sacrificed to a supreme deity, perhaps as a way of petitioning help for the hunt. We know that hunters tracked menacing bears high into the Alps (scaling peaks up to eight thousand feet), and the healed wounds on some bear skeletons make it clear that these animals did not die easily. Supernatural help would have been most welcome.

Another theory disputes the presence of deities in early paleolithic cultic belief and argues that the neat placement of the bear bones probably expresses a desire to ensure renewal of the game. If they considered bone the quintessence of life, the hunters might have thought that preserving and honoring bear bone would generate new bear life. That would also explain the taboo against breaking bones that we find in recent archaic cultures. For instance, up to recent times Chugach Eskimos of Alaska would leave the skull of a bear they had slain muzzle-down in the spot where it died, thinking this would cause it to be reborn (in the skull resided the bear's "soul"—an animating principle that was a miniature of the whole).

An interesting example from the European Alpine caves concerns the skull of a young brown bear that died about twenty thousand years ago. Its incisors and canines had been filed but its molars left intact. This practice matches that of other archaic peoples who celebrate bear festivals, such as the Ainu of Japan: they would file the teeth of a young bear caught for sacrifice so as to prevent it from biting its keepers. The Ainu sacrifice itself was both a petition for bountiful hunts and a reverence toward a totemic ancestor, for the bear was called "grandfather" or "fur-father" (a *totem* is a representation, usually of an animal, with which a tribe or clan identifies). Thus the sacrifice blended a sense that game-life came from an unseen source with a sense that human and animal lives were intimately linked (perhaps even derived from a common ancestry).

Another ritualistic focus of paleolithic culture was representations of the female form. Across a considerable swatch of European geography, researchers have found statues of

26

mature, usually pregnant women, their faces left blank and their feet unformed. They range in height from five to twenty-five centimeters and are carved in bone, ivory, or stone. A subclass, whose most famous member is the "Venus of Wilendorf," depicts a sort of Great Mother: fat, with wavy hair, stick arms and hands, and enormous bosom. Another subclass are pendants or amulets that seem to be abstract, almost geometrical representations of breasts, buttocks, or vulvas. The best conjecture is that these latter figures were considered stimuli to fertility. The domestic context in which many such figures have been found in the Ukraine suggests that the statuettes may have functioned as representations of tutelary spirits in a family-oriented cult. Their tapered or unformed feet are explainable if the figures were made to be set in wall niches. Hunting tribes of northern Asia still carve similar female forms (called *dzuli*), which represent the ancestors from whom all present tribal members have originated. The ancestral statuettes receive wheat flour and fat after any successful hunt.

Since microscopic examination of some of the tiniest female figures has revealed minute markings, the current hypothesis is that they were a lunar or solar calendar notation in the service of increasing fertility. Other statues have holes in their heads, perhaps to hold flowers, leaves, or feathers. One explanation for such adornment is that it links human fertility with that of vegetative or animal nature.

The similarity in statues from such a wide geographical area (France to Siberia) suggests both a remarkable degree of unity in Eurasian paleolithic culture and a remarkable consensus about the importance, indeed the venerability, of the feminine. The Great Mother theme that later agricultural cultures stressed very likely had a considerable background. The Mother was not only the source of crops but also of animal and human life. Furthermore, the layout of the paleolithic village (assuming that a village excavated in Siberia is representative) suggests that the early hunters organized

27

much of their world in terms of a female-male bipolarity. In this Siberian village half the town was male quarters and half was female. (The fact that these halves were, respectively, right and left also is interesting, for other archaic world-views, such as the Chinese, associated the left with the female, or *yin*, half of nature's composition.) Finally, cave paintings from paleolithic times support the notion that female fertility had an almost sacral status. In addition to the hunters' interest in human birth, their observations of animal fertility and their involvement in nature's rhythms of fallow and full would have stimulated them to think of the world as a giant organism both issuing life and taking it back.

By the Aurignacian period (twenty thousand years ago), hunters of eastern Europe and western Siberia had settled along the waterways that dotted the migratory paths of animals such as the mammoth. In the cold winters of this area, hunting was impossible, and so the tribes had to become far-sighted; they had to ration their supplies if they were to get through the long months. And if, as Maringer (pp. 158-59) thinks, much of such provisioning fell to the women, women probably gained a boost in status. That would have given feminine sacrality a base broader than simple child-bearing, and it would dovetail with indications that women partici-pated in the hunters' religious rituals. One such indication is the striping on two Siberian female figurines. Current conjecture is that it represents the animal markings on skins that the women used during shamanistic rituals.

Since we shall deal with shamanism momentarily, the point here is simply to insure that the orientation of a paleolithic cult toward fertility not lose the small nuance that the data allow: most likely the tribe's full "economic" and mythopoeic (story-making) experience lies behind these figurines. Finally, from this Aurignacian period we should tag a motif that will reappear at the rise of agriculture: women's religious prominence was in part a function of a more sedentary life-style. When paleolithic peoples sequestered themselves for near-hibernation, women apparently had important roles. When paleolithic peoples spent most of their time hunting, women probably had auxiliary functions.

Shamanism

The foremost monograph on shamanism (*Shamanism,* by Mircea Eliade) defines it as "archaic techniques of ecstasy." Shamanism is not so much a religion, then, as an orientation or set of practices that has served many different mores and gods. It arises at this juncture because all indications are that it goes back to pre–ice-age hunting peoples. For example, the art of Aurignacian cave dwellers in northern Spain and south-western France depicts what are most likely ritual forms of shamanism aimed at enriching the hunt: by sympathetic magic the hunters apparently sought control over their futures. This cave art depicts more than fifty scenes in which persons are dressed in animal skins and seem to be dancing. If we extrapolate from archaic hunting peoples of recent times, we are more than tempted to read a shamanistic exercise into this cave art. Riding their imaginations, the paleolithic hunters, like their latter-day cousins, identified with the animals of the hunt. Perhaps they petitioned or represented a "master of the animals," who had considerable control over the movements of the herds. Perhaps through totems, mime, and dance they acted out ceremonially the release of the animals, the hunt, the death and replenishment of the game. Driven by their great need to have the hunt succeed and by the dynamics of group contagion, they perhaps set up rhythms of singing and stomping that took them out of themselves (in *ec-stasis*) to the realm of the master of the animals, the life of the herd.

We know quite certainly that this is what used to happen to shamanic peoples of recent times, for instance to arctic Eskimos. The Eskimo shaman regularly would beat his drum, lose himself in frenzied dance, chew great wads of tobacco— all in order to free his spirit for a "flight" to the gods. For coastal Eskimos that flight often was a descent to the undersea realm of Sedna, mistress of the sea animals. For other shamanic peoples it was an ascent to a heavenly realm, where they could petition divine help—not just for the hunt but also for curing illnesses, healing tribal conflicts, and so on. How much of such a full shamanic complex the paleolithic hunters possessed, we cannot say. But the evidence of their full humanity, and the evidence of ecstatic proclivities among hunting peoples the world over, combine to suggest that paleolithic hunters went out of themselves to the forces they imagined were in charge of their fate. Clued by the cave paintings, we can guess that those forces especially concerned animal fertility.

The art of the paleolithic cave dwellers also evidences considerable technical skill. From twenty thousand to ten thousand years ago, human beings clearly possessed a keen eye for a sizable number of animals. Since much of the art occurs in deep recesses of the caves, the likelihood is that it related to religious ceremonies for which rather awe-inspiring depth and darkness were suitable. Moreover, a remarkable feature of some of the paintings is their "x-ray" vision: paleolithic drawings from Europe (and also from North America, India, and Australia) depict these animals' skeletons and internal organs. Surely the artists learned some of this "science" by experimentation—dissection, for instance. But it also seems significant that recent hunters regularly attribute to shamans the ability to see the very essence of life and bodily structure. Eskimo shamans, for example, claim this ability, and among them steady gazing at bones—skulls especially—is a prime initiatory exercise. The x-ray vision therefore probably was in part a shamanic-ecstatic facility.

Small side-features of the cave art allow us to conjecture about other features of the early shamans' outlook. In the cave of Trois Frères in France, for instance, was a picture, obviously retouched several times, of a lion with manifest wounds. It is tempting to imagine a scenario in which a tribe was suffering the depredations of a marauding lion and had to go back several times to increase its dosage of ritual-artistic magic. Since other paintings of animals omitted eyes, ears, or horns, it is tempting to think that a shamanic artist tried to tip the odds in favor of his tribe by depriving the prey of organs they needed to wound or to escape the hunters. If the issue is hard historical fact, we must resist these temptations. But if the issue is trying to picture what it was like to live by hunting wild animals with only crude weapons we ought almost to indulge them. Minimally such a practice stimulated an acute imagination. Just as drawing large teats on the picture of a mare might help her nursing abilities, so depriving a painted lion of an ear might help the hunter sneak up on it. In the sorely trying circumstances of paleolithic peoples, any help was welcome.

Neolithic Farmers and the Goddess

About 8000 B.C.E. the earth's temperature warmed, the glaciers receded, and the mesolithic era began. Culturally there was no abrupt change from paleolithic patterns, but rather a slow evolution. True, agriculture did get under way during the mesolithic era, and such technological developments as the use of the bow and the building of boats. The findings of archaeologists at sites such as Stillmoor (near Hamburg, Germany) show, however, that the changes from paleolithic hunting to neolithic farming were not linear but circular or overlapping. At Stillmoor researchers found the skeletons of twelve reindeer that had been submerged in a lake by placing heavy stones in their abdomens. Hypothetically speaking, these remains represent a mesolithic offering of the "first fruits" of a hunt. At the end of the Ice Age the changed climatic conditions had lessened the game animals and so made a successful hunt more precious. Since tribes then had to supplement their diets, they probably moved to lakeside sites such as Stillmoor to concentrate on fishing. In the more settled life-style that followed they could also concentrate on a rough sort of agricultural research. Negatively and positively, then, the mesolithic changes pointed the way to farming.

31

The beds of the lake at Stillmoor have yielded all sorts of offerings—flints, stone carvings, bone carvings, and so on—that record the thousands of years when culture changed from paleolithic to neolithic. Similarly the rock art of southern Spain and the carved pebbles of Mas d'Azil, a cave in the French Pyrenees, show highly stylized, abstract symbols that may have figured in the ancestor veneration that the mesolithic peoples developed. These pebbles resemble the *tjurungas* that native Australians have used as "ancestor stones," and as native Australians learned in their initiatory rites, the *tjurunga* is an ancestor's mystical body. At the outreach of our imaginative reconstruction, we can guess that mesolithic hunters recalled a paradise time, the Ice Age, when the game was abundant and ancestors flourished. Such ancestors easily could have become more-than-human figures who might help their straitened successors. The pebbles, then, would have concretized petitions and links with a golden past—characteristic of ancestor veneration everywhere. If today tales of gasoline at 27.9 cents a gallon have the ring of a paradise lost, imagine how tales of the woolly mammoth that could feed sixty persons would ring to mesolithic ears.

We know from archaeologists' findings that in the area that became Palestine, mesolithic peoples harvested wild cereals with stone sickles and ground seeds with a mortar and phallus-like pestle. These practices suggest a tie between human fertility and crops, as paleolithic evidences suggest ties between human fertility and animals. Moreover, remains from both Palestine and Europe indicate a mesolithic practice of head-hunting or cannibalism. This custom complicates any simple thesis that prehistoric human beings always reverenced life. The current theory is that archaic persons cut off heads and ate brains because they hoped thereby to appropriate vital powers (which they located in the head).

On the whole, sacrificing living things (including living humans) is more characteristic of crop-cultivators than of hunters. The latter seem to kill only for food, as though they wanted to restrict the use of their basic means of survival to the minimum. Indeed, even necessary killing produces in hunters a significant uneasiness (perhaps because they fear avenging animal spirits), and so they often beg a victim's pardon, deny responsibility for the act by claiming that the arrow wandered off-line, and so on. In the mesolithic increase of ritual killing, then, we find a significant sign that the changes from a nomadic hunting life to a more sedentary gathering and cultivating life were producing inner transformations of great moment. More deeply immersed in an agricultural rhythm of dying and rising, mesolithic peoples conjoined death and life more intimately than paleolithic hunters had.

Between 9000 B.C.E. and 3000 B.C.E. the mesolithic era gave way to the neolithic (the time varied according to the geographical area). From the rude technology that existed at the beginning of this relatively brief transition period there arose, in an almost unique spurt of creativity, such epochal developments as pottery making, trading, the domestication of many animals (sheep, goats, pigs, dogs), the perfection of a lunar calendar (whose roots went back perhaps fifteen thousand years earlier), and the rise of fortified towns and cities (ca. 7000 B.C.E.). But the greatest innovation, which provided the basis for most other neolithic change, was the development of agriculture. By mastering a deliberate cultivation of cereals, tubers, and roots about nine thousand years ago, people of the Middle East made it possible for communities to feed themselves well, increase their populations, and even produce a surplus that could either free some community members for "nonproductive" work or function as exchangeable "wealth."

Religiously, the rise of agriculture led to a shift in focus. Whereas hunters had viewed the ultimate powers that held their fates in terms of the animals on which their economies pivoted, planters viewed such powers in terms of their decisive ties to plant life. As this shift unfolded its implications, the

33

great mysteries of human birth, sexuality, death, afterlife, suffering, and joy were transposed into a new, rhythmic key. The solidarity between human beings and a cyclically growing plant life meant that human beings more decisively inserted themselves into the turning of the earth's seasons. The alternation of fallow and full, withered and flowing, dry and rainy, came to color the planters' consciousness. It even came to color the planters' gods, for with the rise of agriculture we find more distinct deities who themselves die and rise up again. To honor such deities and set themselves in the earth's rhythms, farmers created festivals that celebrated planting and harvesting, the new year and high summer. They kept a firm moral discipline through the growing periods, but at the end of the year they legitimized a period of orgiastic wantonness—a scattering of creative energies like the chaos that nature itself occasionally visited on them (in storms, floods, and the like).

In India this correlation between human life and cyclical nature appears to have stimulated what became a doctrine of reincarnation. Just as vegetative life passes through cycles of dying and being reborn, so may the human vital force. Indeed, the world itself may pulsate in gigantic periods of rest and creativity (*kalpas*), as though it were a primal organism. In China findings show that neolithic farming helped restructure early peoples' perceptions of space. Since farmers no longer wandered extensively, they tended to conceive the space that surrounded their living quarters as a sort of circumference. Many of their huts were circular, and if the Mongolian *yurt* is related to this neolithic re-perception of space, the enclosure of a circular form was balanced by an opening in the roof to heaven. The transactions involved make our reconstruction uncertain, but it would be interesting indeed if farming peoples' greater ties to the earth inspired their need for a balancing transcendence (opening the roof of the mind to "higher" things).

Agricultural Myths

By carefully employing myths from archaic cultivators of recent times, we can retroject onto early farmers certain likely views of agriculture itself. Generally the recent myths attribute plant life to a divine source: seeds from heaven, the marriage of Father Sky and Mother Earth, a deity's sweat (or excreta or corpse). In such attribution they are saying that food plants are sacred—come from ultimate reality, from the bones of holy originality. Further, since food plants are sacred, eating food plants is a way of communing with divinity; by ingesting the god's "body" one partakes of divine life.

A myth from eastern Indonesia summarizes these themes and adds a further precision: the origin of plant life is the immolation of a goddess, Hainuwele. (See Campbell pp. 173-76.) This immolation occurred in a primal past time, before the world came to have its present structure. At that time primordial beings called *dema* lived on earth in various forms: as deities, humans, plants, and animals. One day a dema-man named Ameta found a coconut on a wild boar's tusk. He planted it as he had been directed in a dream, and in six days it became a flowering tree. In cutting some of the tree's flower, Ameta cut his finger as well and spilled his blood on a blossom. Nine days later he found on the blossom a baby girl, whom he wrapped in coconut fronds and carried home. In three more days this girl, whom he had named Hainuwele ("coconut branch"), was marriageable. So for nine nights she stood at the dancing place of the Maro festival and gave gifts to the dancers (as a sign of her availability?). But on the ninth night some men dug a pit, threw Hainuwele in, and danced on her grave. When Ameta learned that she had been murdered, he recovered her body and cut it into many pieces. He then buried the pieces in several different places. At those places soon arose new varieties of plants, especially tubers, which ever since have been humanity's main food.

35

The continuation of the myth shows the connection between plants, food, and death that many farming cultures have intuited. When he chopped up Hainuwele's corpse, Ameta kept back her arms. He took them to Satene, a dema-deity, and from them she made a door. Calling the dancers, she told them that because of their having killed Hainuwele, she (Satene) would no longer live in their midst, henceforth they would only be able to meet her by passing through the door of death. Thus death came to human beings as the reverse side of the act by which their foodstuffs arose. (This myth is actually even more complex: Satene has the dancers pass through the door; those who do so remain human beings, while those who refuse become the various subhuman species—fish, pigs, birds. Thus the myth also functions as a creation account, explaining how the various kinds of life arose.)

At the death of Hainuwele primal time ended, and the sort of imperfect mortal existence that modern persons know began. Now human beings have to struggle to keep death at bay. They have to labor for food and secure new life through sexual relations.

Archetypes and the Goddess

One characteristic of archaic peoples is that they derive from their myths a sense of living in the pattern of divine archetypes. Current arrangements, whether socio-economic, familial, or religious, derive from primordial actions that took place before or at the dawn of this present world order. Usually the actors in these archetypal happenings are deities, or at least ancestors of heroic scale. When it comes time to carry out a present action—for example, harvesting this season's crop of tubers—an archaic tribe will tend to make a ceremony that reenacts the primal paradigm. In the case of east Indonesian culture, this means launching the harvest by a recitation, dramatization, dance, or the like that brings the Hainuwele story vividly into the present.

36

Moreover, if a myth is central to a people's understanding of its present situation, the story may focus, not only the specific events that now move in its shadow (e.g., harvesting), but also other events that draw upon its clarification of primal forces. Thus, the Hainuwele myth might center a marriage ceremony, in which sex and procreation are at issue. It might center a puberty rite, in which adult capacity to work and reproduce is at stake. It might even be an ingredient in funeral services, if it provided the people their main understanding of death. In the compact world-view of archaic persons, sexuality, death, and vegetative life are forces that swarm together. One comprehensive myth can therefore make up a culture's core. (The situation is not wholly dissimilar in more differentiated cultures. Insofar as the death and resurrection of Jesus is the axis of the Christian story, it shapes all the prime moments of truly Christian culture or communal life.)

Since it has this crucial reference to archetypes, the archaic religious mind lays great stress on memory. At each time for celebration, each occasion when the tribe must solemnize a happening of the personal or natural life-cycle, the archaic tendency is to go back *in illud tempus*: to the primal time when the world received its present shape. As a result, there is a further tendency to think that "in the beginning" things were better. Relations between human beings and the controlling powers were more intimate, ancient ancestors were giants. By comparison, our present generation seems puny, lacking the powers, longevity, and creative might that our ancient ancestors had because of their closeness to the primal time. The beginnings, then, were a golden age or a paradise. They were how things ought to be. The present age is by contrast fallen. Physically, morally, and ontologically (in our being), we are children who experience less grace. To try to retrieve what measure of grace (favor with the ultimate powers and harmony in our own living) we can, we must above all become people who *remember*. Only by attuning ourselves to the archetypal happenings, through both our tribe's ceremonial life and our personal efforts at quiet reflectiveness, can we hope to live realistically and deal with the world as it truly is. The greatest enemy of human wisdom and prosperity, therefore, is forgetfulness. The serpent in the human bosom is amnesia. Each ritual storytelling or dance aims at defanging amnesia and returning us to how things really are.

In the case of Hainuwele, which we are suggesting retains something of the mesolithic cultivators' mind, memory travels back to the time when agriculture received its sanction as a holy way of life. Each retelling of the Hainuwele story approved again the cycle of death and rebirth into which an agricultural existence inserts human beings. Though there are elements in the story that we moderns would expect to receive a clearer moral interpretation (such as the reason Hainuwele was chosen to suffer the price of agriculture's beginning and what reward she gets in return), the main point is admirably clear: by a certain "fall," agriculture and death begot the present world order. Ever since, the price of the goods of agriculture is the evils of mortality.

Many other archaic peoples express a similar understanding. The myth of the stone and the banana, which is also from the Indonesian cultural area, puts this idea even more succinctly than the myth of Hainuwele. Once upon a time the gods sent down to human beings a stone. Turning it over and contemplating its uses, human beings decided to send it back: it was too hard, too inert. Surely the gods could come up with something better. So the gods sent down a banana. That was more like it: something pleasant to behold, easy to handle, good to eat. But just when human beings were congratulating themselves on their shrewd bargaining, the gods delivered a solemn rescript. Because the people had chosen the banana, human beings henceforth would be like t: vulnerable and subject to death. Had they chosen what the gods first offered—the stone—they would have been invulnerable and immortal; the present order therefore resulted from

38

humanity's failure to trust divinity and live gratefully. It came as a "fall" into the vegetative cycles of nature.

We should stress at this point that, strictly speaking, the origin of agriculture usually does not involve a *sacrifice*. (See Jensen, pp. 166-68.) The dema-reality in plants or human beings that passes down to death is not destroyed as a holy offering to ultimate powers. Rather, the dema-reality has assumed (for reasons finally out of the sight of cultivators) the present "economy" of the vegetative seasons, and human beings can only hope that their participation in this economy will bring them good fortune. They can only hope as well that they can relate across death to their ancestors, who return to the dema community (go through the door to Satene) profitably. By *eating* the foodstuffs that the dema-deities animate, human beings can achieve an intimate communion with ultimacy before death. Thus each human meal is almost a sacrament—an active sign that mediates the "grace" of union with ultimacy.

On the other hand, it seems clear that the cultivators' concern with food-by-death, even more than the hunters' concern, did provide a rationale for sacrifice. Whatever its ties to the conceptions of earlier hunting cultures, the cultivators' focus on the original immolation of a deity opened the door to the practice of immolating animals or even human beings at times of high celebration or petition. To pay the agricultural "law" of life from death its debt, farmers would let blood flow into the earth as a sort of replenishment of the original power-stuff that launched the economy of cultivation. Further, in circumstances under which severe famine seems unlikely, sufficient evidences of prehistoric cannibalism exist to force scholars to take a hard look at sacrificing life for the maintenance of crops. The cruelty that arose among later agricultural peoples, who tortured victims and sent retinues of slaves or companions to death along with rulers, probably was a debasement of original practices. (See Jensen, pp. 162-206.) Nonetheless, something in the agriculturalists' new relation to nature (perhaps their distance from the violent killing by which hunters lived), made them focus on the intertwining of life, life-nourishment, and death. The cultivators' reverence for life therefore occasionally took the dangerous form of sacrificing blood today for fertility tomorrow.

Finally, we find that by neolithic times agricultural peoples had clarified the "ultimate powers" behind the cycle of nature's dying and rising and found a Great Goddess, often a Great Mother. From the Middle East to southeastern Europe, archaeologists have found remains of a cult that included food offerings to a female deity. Neolithic representations of the Great Mother in both fields and homes developed the paleolithic concern with female fertility, but the emphasis shifted from the Mother as source of animal life to her personification as Mother Earth. It is likely that women's primacy in agriculture (either in discovering agriculture or in doing most of the actual farming) stimulated this development, but basically it depended on the parallel between the birth of children from a human mother and the birth of crops from the earth.

Characteristically, the dense archaic world-view runs themes together, using a logic more symbolic than deductive. Thus it is not surprising that neolithic women's economic importance and the agriculturalists' stress on the Great Goddess combined to generate female political power. For example, societies of the neolithic period often show signs of having been matrilocal (a couple would settle in the woman's home area) and matrilineal (the line of descent would come through the mother). The prominence that female fertility assumed at the rise of agriculture is all the more intelligible if tribes still were hazy about the biology of reproduction. Like Mother Earth, the human mother seemed to procreate independently, from her own resources. Later developments, through which the roles of males become clearer, probably led to the heterosexual, hierogamic (sacred marriage) practices that were prominent in fertility cults like those of Canaan, against which the Hebrew prophets inveighed in the eighth century B.C.E. By that time plowing, sowing seed, watering and the like were assimilated to human fertilization. Then the farmer (increasingly male?) helped Father Sky fertilize Mother Earth, extending to Mother Earth the solicitude he would offer a pregnant woman.

The Megalith Builders

Against a backdrop of neolithic concern with vegetative themes like these rise up the astounding "great stones" (*megaliths*) of such areas as Stonehenge. Like the toys of a giant child, they are scattered across southern Spain, Portugal, and France, to the western coast of England, the outreach of Iceland, and the northern realms of Denmark and Sweden. They originated from approximately 4000 B.C.E. to 2000 B.C.E. (the earliest ones therefore predated the Egyptian pyramids by a thousand years), served as colossal tombs, temples, and monuments, and still await complete explanation.

Megaliths come in several shapes. The *menhir* is a long stone (often twenty to thirty feet) set in the ground vertically. When menhirs are arranged in a circle, semicircle, or ellipse, they are called a *cromlech*, of which Stonehenge is the most famous example. If they are arranged in parallel rows, we speak of an *alignment*. The alignment at Carnac in Brittany consisted of 2,935 menhirs on land 4,000 yards long. From a distance it looked like an army drawn up in drill formation; up close, the areas between the rows formed avenues for ceremonial processions. Finally, a *dolmen* (in simplest form) is a huge capstone supported by three or four other stones. When covered with earth, these supporting stones formed a roomlike burial enclosure, capable of holding hundreds of bodies. The Soto dolmen near Seville, Spain, is 68 feet long. The granite stones that form its front are 11 feet by 10 feet by 2½ feet, and they weigh about 21 tons. It is likely these stones were transported at least 20 miles, since that seems to be the distance to the nearest quarry.

The obvious question is What were the megalith builders up to? What benefit could they have had in mind when they set to the immense labor their constructions entailed? To try to answer this question we have to back up slightly. First, by such methods as radiocarbon dating and dendrochronology (dating by reference to tree rings), scholars have arrived at a date for the rise of European megalith building that correlates with the rise of a critical mass of population and a considerable economic sophistication. Hypothesizing, they suggest that population pools too large to be organized efficiently would have been subdivided into smaller units, quite likely along family lines. (See Renfrew, pp. 120-46.) Supporting this hypothesis, historians of engineering have explained how the neolithic peoples built their megalithic structures, making it clear that these people had both a good-sized labor pool and considerable sophistication about pulleys, rollers, and so on. Furthermore, it appears that megaliths everywhere were built in locales that would have attracted large numbers of people (for instance, places that had lakes for fish and game, as well as good farmland). By contrast, nonmegalithic lands probably were less attractive.

In a context of full population, the people would have needed not only to employ resources and creativity but also to establish clear boundary lines, firm subcommunal identities, and peaceful relations among neighbors (perhaps by creating "families" of relatively equal strength). If so, it was a magnificent stroke, a leap of genius, to establish a group's identity through the common labor and the common honoring of ancestors that megalithic building entailed. To support such a hypothetical explanation, of course, we must find good indications that the megalith builders did intend to honor their ancestors. So let us consider indications that scholars working in this area advance. (See Eliade, 1978a, pp. 114-24; Daniel, *passim*.)

From the art work of the megaliths themselves, the burial remains that many megalithic sites have yielded, and ethnological parallels with stone builders of more recent times, it seems likely that stone served the prehistoric builders as a medium for expressing their beliefs about the dead, their veneration of ancestors, and their orientation toward the Great Goddess. As we saw in the touching little story of the stone and the banana, archaic peoples of recent times have seized upon the hardness of rock—its invulnerability and durability—to symbolize what stands over against mortal humanity. On the one hand, rock clearly can seem inferior to plant, animal, or human life, for it has no movement or creativity. On the other hand, the manifest imperfections of the mode of existence we call living led some archaic peoples to imagine divinity as a stonelike inertness. That is, a perfect mode of existence would not entail the change, suffering, and death that the human mode does. We see this notion in some yogic speculation, in which the goal is a self-sufficiency that carries one beyond ordinary consciousness. We see it also in some Asian speculation, such as that of Japanese Buddhists, that finds nature a more perfect expression of ultimate reality (the Buddha-nature) than human beings because nature struggles less for its completion. Without such conceptual clarity, neolithic stone builders probably were expressing a similar conviction. To represent the more-than-human, and distance themselves from the immersion in the cycles of life and death that agriculture had brought, they seized upon great, heavy, seemingly imperishable stones.

The agriculturalists had numerous reasons to believe that something may well survive the corruptible human body at death. As the seed that is buried in the ground at planting only apparently dies, springing to new life after the barren winter of germination, so too perhaps with the human vital principle. In India, as we suggested earlier, this observation developed into a theory of reincarnation: the vital principle returns to animate a new body. For the megalith builders it seems to have taken a different direction. They associated the vital principle, and so the postmortem existence of ancestors, with stone. As a result, they had the ancestors available to them almost permanently in the megaliths.

Moreover, insofar as stones fit the notion of Mother Earth, being found in her depths like infants in the womb or appearing to be her ribs and skeletal structure, they completed a certain circle. Both plant life and the more "real" life of stones came from the Mother. The logic of this relation may seem strange to us, but the archaic mind of Amerindians, Africans, and Australians suggests that the megalithic builders could easily have made such an illation. At any rate, there are clear indications that many of the megaliths functioned as ceremonial sites for worship of the Great Goddess. They also functioned as places where the ancestors (who were with the Goddess as stones) could be venerated. Thus fertility, immortality, and help with present needs all came together in the megalithic cult.

A most impressive prehistoric megalithic site that concretizes many of these themes is the Maltese archipelago off the coast of Sicily. There before 3000 B.C.E., people of what seems to have been a rather unpretentious farming culture built grandiose temples to the Goddess. Although their own housing was probably of simple clay, they erected stone womblike rooms with life-size statues, altars, paintings, and delicately worked facades. Very likely they had a well-organized clergy, with both priests and priestesses, and their cult seems to have included both animal sacrifice and the tending of a sacred fire before the Goddess. In one statue the Goddess is about eight feet high, corpulent, and has a flounced, pleated skirt of stone. She is seated, and under her skirt shelter many tiny human beings, as though she were protecting them (like a medieval Madonna). (See Von Cles-Reden, pp. 94-96.)

The mythology of the Maltese Goddess seems to have attributed the strength to assemble the great stones (some weighing fifty tons) to the magical power of a nursing mother.

44

The shrine obviously drew sick persons seeking a cure, and probably it also offered rites for divining the future. People apparently would sleep there, hoping to receive a communication from the Mother in a dream. Archaeologists have found a clever contrivance by which sounds carry along special moldings of the walls, probably to make "revelations" possible. Also on Malta is the Hypogeum, a megalithic structure distinctive because it functioned as both a temple and a tomb. Its underground patterns are labyrinthine and womblike, as if to encourage the notion that one is in the entrails of the Mother. Excavators have removed the bones of more than seven thousand persons, a discovery that shows that the Hypogeum housed no small-scale burial operation.

The menhirs appear to have functioned in fertility ceremonies that stressed the phallus, as astronomical observatories, and as burial sites for local chieftains. Since they are erect, it is easy to see how they become both symbols of male fertility and substitute bodies for eminent dead persons. Possibly the astronomical observations for which menhirs served were linked with a fertility interest, in that agricultural peoples often considered certain times (e. g., the solstice or the time of an eclipse) propitious for planting. Some of the menhirs are paired sexually, and one explanation is that they represented the Goddess and her consort.

The fertility overtones to European menhirs continued through historic times, prompting much church opposition to pagan practices, such as women rubbing themselves against the stones when they wanted to conceive. In addition, a Christian mythology grew up around some menhirs, such as a pair in Corsica that in popular thought represented a priest and nun who had become lovers and tried to flee monastic life. God turned them to stone as a warning to others who might entertain such sinful notions.

Two of the most impressive menhir sites are Carnac in Brittany and Stonehenge in England. Both seem to have hosted processions, dances, and sacrifices on a grand scale.

The menhirs of Carnac form avenues capable of accommodating thousands of marchers. Scholars conjecture that behind Stonehenge lie such sociological developments as the rise of a more powerful chiefdom and a more professional priestly caste. Certainly the creation and use of Stonehenge required considerable organization, and the likeliest explanation for the astronomical sightings that one can make using its menhirs is that a group of priest-scholars worked with them regularly. The degree of astronomical precision one can achieve in this "laboratory" is so astounding that it argues for a long-term, perhaps even a hereditary, vocation to record data and interpret them. For an agricultural people, all information about the seasons is precious. If comparisons with more recent archaic peoples who have made impressive astronomical observations and calendars hold, we can conjecture that the people of Stonehenge possessed a degree of social complexity between that of the Hopi and the Maya Indians.

Until the turn of the twentieth century, megalithic construction continued in Indonesia and Melanesia, where the builders clearly focused on life after death and the ancestors. Up to recent times also, Irish peasants referred to speaking-stones and stones with magical fertility powers. In twentieth-century Estonia a stone axe under the nuptial bed was supposed to insure sturdy offspring, and in nineteenth-century Brittany stone hammers were used to dispatch infirm senior citizens to their eternal reward. The great stones therefore root in our deep psychic tendency to associate stone with immortality. Perhaps they carry on today when we build great cathedrals and mausoleums.

The Wonder of Metal

Early peoples probably first encountered metal when it fell from the sky in meteorites. Neolithic groups made crude tools and weapons from such metal, whose impression on them we can gather from the names they gave their implements:

"thunderstones," "God's axes," and "thunderbolt teeth."
(See Eliade, 1978*a*, p. 52.) The scarcity of metal made such
tools precious, and they probably served ritual uses more than
practical ones. We know from later times that the Aztecs,
Incas, and Mayas of Central and South America actually
valued knives made of meteoric metal more highly than knives
made of gold, and the Eskimos of Greenland were still
working meteoric metal in the nineteenth century. In all
likelihood, therefore, prehistoric peoples stood in awe of this
strange substance that came from the sky in a shower of fire.
As with the ores they discovered in the earth, they probably
began to work the meteorites like stone, discovering their
special properties only slowly.

At any rate, metal sufficiently fascinated the archaic mind
to generate a rich cluster of myths, rituals, and taboos. Gold
early became a symbol of immortality and divinity, silver
weapons early carried an aura of invincibility, and iron goods
could protect their bearer from devils, witches, storms,
illness, the evil eye, crop failure, abortion, and more. On the
darker side, both gold and silver became associated with
greed, jealousy, and death, while iron stood accused of
poisoning the soil, destroying peace, and being a bearer of
death (the last two accusations clearly deriving from its use in
weaponry). Inevitably, before long the ambivalence toward
metals that these associations reveal attached to those who
mined, smelted, or cast metals. For instance, the blacksmith
became a mysterious figure who could increase a people's
measure of weal or woe. (Since iron was being mined,
smelted, and worked into tools or weapons in the twelfth
century B.C.E., the symbols it generated could be highly
archaic. Moreover, some scholars argue that the technology
involved in neolithic pottery, which was fired in kilns, would
have sufficed for smelting copper. That theory supports
evidences from Balkan sites that potter-smiths worked ores as
early as 4000 B.C.E.. The objects found there also indicate that
pottery and metal working served a cult of the Great Goddess,

for voluptuous female images abound, bedecked with copper (amulets, rings, and bracelets.)

Another suggestion that archaic religion was intimately associated with early metallurgy comes from the folklore of elves, saints, gods, and goddesses that we find surrounding metallurgy everywhere. Such folklore probably roots in the basic notion that all metal—meteoric, surface, or mined—possesses some sacral power. The meteoric metals share in the power of Father Sky, while the telluric (earth) metals share in the power of Mother Earth. So strong was the association between Mother Earth and fertility that metals too came to be considered her children. A mythology and symbolism developed to explain the (living) metals' sexuality and fertility: hard, black male ores fertilize soft, red female ones, and so forth. A common background theme was that heavenly or volcanic fire impregnated Mother Earth, causing her to bear metals in the first place. Metals required a long gestation period, and ancient Indians and Chinese both believed that, were they left alone to come to full term, all metals finally would be gold. The notion was still current in nineteenth-century Spain that when a mine appears to be running out, one need only leave it alone for a while, since Mother Earth will regenerate its metals in time.

Because of their work within the womb of Mother Earth, miners became special persons, as smiths became special persons because of their work with Mother Earth's children. Metallurgical processes were considered a way of speeding up the gestation that would have gone on in the earth, so those who carried out such processes had to protect themselves with amulets, rituals, prayers, and the like. The smith was not a prestigious figure among nomadic peoples, but for agriculturalists he became so exalted that stories developed of the First Smith, who brought to earth tools for cultivation or even played a role in creation. As the reverse of this exaltation, many peoples feared the smith as a polluter of land, someone whose name was not to be mentioned after dark.

Other peoples believed that intercourse with a smith's wife would bring insanity, defective offspring, or death in one's next battle. Perhaps such intercourse was a temptation, for smiths regularly followed rigorous regimes of abstinence from sexual relations. To fire the kiln or cast the metal "purely," they had to stay apart from women, sometimes for as long as two months. In most places a woman could never enter a smithy, above all if she were pregnant, and if a smith were to divorce a woman, her very life could be in peril. Not surprisingly, then, people were reluctant to let their daughters marry smiths.

When the smith's role came to full efflorescence, he was credited with clairvoyance, prophecy, crime detection, exorcism, healing, and even preventive medicine (he could immunize a person by hardening him or her like iron). In Africa his religious preparations made him the rival of the tribal chieftain or shaman, and the spread of the smith's scope finally made him one of humankind's first self-employed technologists, working full time and bartering his products for food, clothing, and shelter. (See Forbes, pp. 53-54.)

Itinerant smiths, who probably came originally from India, added fortune-telling and musical entertainment to their repertory, becoming "Gypsies." In the popular mind their powers came from dwarfs, the dead, or the devil, and so they were much feared (suspicion of Gypsies has continued in Europe to the present day). In Java the smith was equivalently a priest. In Angola the smith's hammer was worshiped in the cult of Mother Earth. Other African areas had practices such as carrying a smith's anvil in procession like a bride (if blessed by a powerful smith, she would bear many "children"). Again and again one finds that the smith's powers overflow to his paraphernalia: his tools, furnace, and so on. The furnace, perhaps because of its womblike structure, focused a demand for sexual purity. On occasion it also focused a sense that the "life" of a new metal demands another life in exchange—even a human life. How grisly this actually became is hard to say, but Chinese folklore tells of husband-and-wife smiths whose

49

efforts to fuse metals led to their immolation. Other tales speak of a smith who consecrated a finely wrought sword with the blood of his two sons, of the sacrifice of cocks by African smiths, and on and on. The life being born in the furnace could be demanding.

Indian myths also related the smith to sacrifice and to the displeasure of the gods. When Sing-bonga, the supreme god of Asurs, was displeased by the smoke from the smelting furnaces and could not get humans to stop polluting his air, he came to earth incognito and tricked metal workers into entering their furnaces, where he had them burned alive. (See Eliade, 1978a, p. 65.) This dark theme exemplifies a general tendency to regard the age of iron as debased—filled with malevolent gods, giants, and demons. Perhaps the warfare that followed on the use of metal was projected back to the age of its discovery. At any rate, some cultures thought metal per se evil, and so indeed capable of demanding human sacrifice.

By early historical times, metallurgy had gained a regular seat in the pantheon. Thus the Indian god Indira spills his seed as gold, the Persian god Gayomart is assassinated and from his body come all kinds of metals, the Roman god Vulcan and the Greek god Hephaestus are wily smiths. In Scandinavia, Japan, and other places it is the same: metal merits a place in the family of gods. By association with fire, peoples without a clear pantheon put smiths in the same nest as shamans (who stir up "inner heat"). Even medieval Christian folklore made the devil and Jesus masters of fire, which somewhat explains the alchemists of medieval Europe, who often worked with religious fervor. Though the church opposed them, their work with metals had such archaic roots that they were able to survive.

Summary: The Prehistoric Religious Mind

We have briefly surveyed the impact of prehistoric hunting, agriculture, megalith building, and metal working. What heritage have they bequeathed us?

From hunters humanity has received a view of the world that we may broadly call shamanic. In this world-view one may go out ecstatically to the powers that control existence, especially the supply of game. Perhaps from Ice-Age times hunters meditated on the awesome fertility of animals, and they probably pictured their gods in animal form. Hunters also were impressed by female powers, and, as we saw, much of their cult seems to have used statuettes in an effort to obtain children or secure easy births.

Agriculture brought a more stable, sedentary situation that eventually gave rise to city life. Religiously, the shift from focusing on animals of the hunt to plants of the field seems to have clarified the link between life and death and to have generated the greater veneration of female sacrality implied in "Mother Earth." Both the megalith builders and the metal workers continued a close association with Mother Earth, the former associating her with ancestor veneration and the latter with mining. By according "life" and "fertility" to stone and metal, megalith builders and metal workers reveal the prime thrust of the prehistoric mind.

Essentially the prehistoric religious mind searched vigorously for *life*, meaning by this stable, long-lasting, fecund power. The prehistoric religious mind became deeply concerned with death because death threatened life. Indeed, this mind often made death the gateway to a stronger life. We must never forget how fragile and perilous existence was for prehistoric peoples: that their concern for fertility—whether of game, crops, or humans— should have been more intense than ours makes a great deal of sense. Since their concern for fertility reverberated through a consciousness that moved by symbols and stories, it could attach itself simultaneously to several different objects. In fact, whatever was awesome, full of power, or fraught with vitality solicited early humans' hopes for fertility and survival. Whatever was sacred (intensely real) might secure fragile human existence, and so it was worth petitioning. At bottom, then, prehistoric peoples

51

have bequeathed us a wonder at the mystery of *life*—a wonder that has played through all later culture and religion. Whether it focused historically on nature, society, the self, or a transcendent God, this wonder opened human beings to beauty. It set them to reflecting about transcience and pain. It kept them to the marrow of being human.

Despite all our technological sophistication, the beginning and beyond of the modern world too remain hidden. Despite all our technological sophistication, none of us twentieth-century folk has ever seen God or come back from the dead. Insofar as these are facts that define life in a human mode, archaic peoples remain our kin. We owe prehistoric archaic peoples thanks for having preserved the human species many times longer than modernity has. If we wished, we might also offer recent archaic peoples thanks for having reminded us what we lose when Mother Earth and the ancestors are so distant that life no longer is full of wonder.

Bibliography

Brown, Peter Lancaster. *Megaliths, Myths, and Men.* New York: Taplinger, 1976.

Campbell, Joseph. *The Masks of God: Primitive Mythology.* New York: Viking, 1970.

Daniel, Glyn. *The Megalith Builders of Western Europe.* New York: Praeger, 1958.

Eliade, Mircea. *A History of Religious Ideas, I: From the Stone Age to the Eleusinian Mysteries.* Chicago: University of Chicago Press, 1978*a.*

———. *The Forge and the Crucible.* 2d ed., paper. Chicago: University of Chicago Press, 1978*b.*

———. *From Primitives to Zen.* New York: Harper & Row, 1967.

———. *Shamanism.* Paper. Princeton: Princeton University Press, 1972.

Forbes, R. J. *Studies in Ancient Technology, Vol. VIII.* Leiden: E. J. Brill, 1964.

Forde-Johnston, J. *Prehistoric Britain and Ireland.* New York: Norton, 1976.

Hawkins, Gerald S. *Beyond Stonehenge.* New York: Harper & Row, 1973.

Herity, Michael and Eogan, George. *Ireland in Prehistory.* London: Routledge & Kegan Paul, 1977.

James, E. O. *Prehistoric Religion.* London: Thames & Hudson, 1957.

Jensen, Adolf E. *Myth and Cult Among Primitive Peoples.* Chicago: University of Chicago Press, 1963.

PREHISTORIC RELIGION

Maringer, Johannes. *The Gods of Prehistoric Man*. New York: Alfred A. Knopf, 1960.

Marsheck, Alexander. *The Roots of Civilization*. New York: McGraw-Hill, 1972.

Piggott, Stuart. *The Neolithic Cultures of the British Isles*. Cambridge: Cambridge University Press, 1970.

Renfrew, Colin. *Before Civilization*. New York: Alfred A. Knopf, 1974.

Singer, Charles, *et al.*, eds. *A History of Technology, Vol. I*. Oxford: Clarendon Press, 1956.

Von Cles-Reden, Sibylle. *The Realm of the Great Goddess: The Story of the Megalith Builders*. Englewood Cliffs: Prentice-Hall, 1962.

Todd, Ian A. *Catal Huyuk in Perspective*. Menlo Park: Cummings, 1976.

Wood, John Edwin. *Sun, Moon, and Standing Stones*. Oxford: Oxford University Press, 1978.

Chapter 2:
Civilizational Religion

The Rise of Civilization

We moderns tend to ascribe civilization to the culture of cities that developed some form of writing. For with writing a people was on the verge of history, in the sense that history depends largely on written records from which one can reconstruct the flow of the past. Cities appear to have arisen in the Middle East around 3000 B.C.E. They depended on a previous town culture (and on the stability, or even prosperity, that agriculture had brought), and they gave rise to denser populations, unified governments, and specialists freed for such non-agricultural enterprises as technological improvements, trade, warfare, and priestly concerns. The previous dependence of cities on town cultures goes back to at least 5500 B.C.E. in Europe, where walled villages of up to a thousand inhabitants existed in the Balkan Peninsula. (See Gimbutas.) That area has yielded numerous temple remains, and signs indicate that around 5300 B.C.E., two millenia before Sumer, it had developed a workable form of writing. Neolithic towns of comparable scale are implied by remains from Poland, Switzerland, Egypt, Jordan, and parts of India and Russia. Our first question is how this movement toward villages and then cities influenced neolithic religion.

Perhaps a good way to make this question concrete is to consider what may well have been the world's first town: Jericho. (See Kenyon, pp. 51-76.) Excavations begun in the

Jordan Valley in 1930 have revealed that Jericho was settled between 10,000 and 7000 B.C.E. It seems to have covered eight to ten acres and to have housed as many as three thousand inhabitants. Though these dates place it before the making of pottery, it was not a nomadic community's temporary settlement, for the houses the people built were substantial (made of bricks of sun-baked clay). They were laid out in lines both utilitarian and aesthetic, with such conveniences as a central courtyard for cooking, plastered walls and floors for easy washing, rush mats, storage bins, and utensils of limestone and flint. What appear to be temple remains indicate a cultic use of stone and also a fertility orientation toward the Mother Goddess. The people of Jericho must have revered their dead, for they preserved skulls in a finely molded plaster that gave them a delicate, lifelike appearance. The walls of this town were built many times, a fact that suggests both a high level of community cooperation and the presence of external enemies. All in all, then, Jericho resembles a prosperous little medieval town, with rich fields outside and numerous amenities inside.

By comparison with the wandering life that prehistoric peoples led before the rise of towns, the new settled existence must have possessed many advantages. Most likely it afforded the chance to develop better food supplies, health care, and traditional customs, all of which would have tended to increase the people's life span and sense of security. Women's roles in the early towns seem to have been important: in addition to their involvement with farming, women probably also worked at the domestication of animals, the development of weaving, and the perfecting of pottery making. Remains from Jarmo (near the border of Iran and Iraq) that date to about 6750 B.C.E. show both a strong Mother Goddess religion and a considerable domestication of animals (90 percent of the animal bones found there are from domesticated species, such as sheep, pigs, and goats). (See Hammond, pp. 18 ff.) The link between a

Mother Goddess religion and the nurture of animals also suggests that women's economic-religious roles were significant. None of the great advances that occurred at this time—discovery of most plant species, use of fertilizer (largely the waste of domestic animals), and food grains—needed great physical strength, while the pig and the snake, both of which served new domestic uses, became symbols of the Goddess (when patriarchal religions overthrew the Goddess cult, the pig and the snake came into the disfavor they have retained to the present time). Town architecture often used such enclosing shapes as the beehive, and early writing such as the Egyptian hieroglyphics referred to towns themselves as "mothers." Thus the period of early town life probably was a good one for women.

Finally, we should note that although town life directly followed on the development of agriculture, it did not completely destroy hunting. Some scholars conjecture that both shepherds and chieftain-kings continued the hunting line. In the best of situations shepherds cooperated with farmers, providing them fertilizer, early warning against the approach of enemies, and so forth. On the other hand, the chieftain-king was an ambiguous figure. The very qualities that made him valuable as a military leader could also make him overbearing. It is likely that the decisive turn to male rule (there are some suggestions that early towns had a council of elders of both sexes—see Mumford, pp. 19; 21-25) came when hunters assumed first protective, and then kingly, positions.

History Begins at Sumer

Around 3200 B.C.E. in southern Mesopotamia (present-day Iraq) the first true civilization arose, that of Sumer. Sumer lay between the Tigris and Euphrates rivers (other rivers—the Nile in Egypt, the Huang-Ho in China, and the Indus in India—also hosted early civilizations), and it developed a rich culture to parallel its rich farmland. The farmland provided agricultural surpluses, which could support a population large enough not only to work the fields but also to drain swamps, develop irrigation systems, and generally expand and upgrade the Sumerians' holdings. This progress produced a buzz of economic activity sufficient to stimulate an efficient way of keeping records—first by pictographic writing, then by cuneiform writing (wedge-shaped impressions with a stylus on clay). Moreover, the bustling prosperity of Sumer attracted artisans of all sorts—metal workers, jewelers, carpenters, and more. It was in Sumer that the wheel was invented, and probably also the plow and the chariot. We can glimpse something of the Sumerian cultural style and the skill and frugality of its carpenters from records that archaeologists have found: three old table tops and four fir boxes were remade into one table, two beds, and one small box.

The physical core of the Sumerian cities was religious: the temple that housed the local god or goddess. Indeed, some historians speculate that cities may have arisen basically as ceremonial centers—aggregations for worship. The temples were major landholders, and therefore tied directly to the economy. For example, records show that the temple of the goddess Bau around 2400 B.C.E. controlled serf-run estates whose grain, fruit, fish, and herbs were sufficient to support about twelve hundred temple employees. Temples provided their own farm equipment, breeding stock, bakers, brewers, wool workers, spinners, weavers, and administrators; they were small-scale corporations. The priests and priestesses who controlled the temple affairs therefore tended to be educated for business administration as well as ritual performance. In effect they were an elite minority—the upper class of the first class-divided society.

The king, who probably was elected in earliest times, owed his position to the gods. Most profoundly he was conceived to be a son of the gods, for his coronation had the motif that he was being born again of the god and goddess of the city, and each New Year festival reaffirmed his divine status. Specifically, each Sumerian New Year involved a sacred

57

marriage, in which the king had intercourse with a priestess who represented the goddess Inanna. Since the king himself represented Dumuzi, Inanna's consort, the intent of the sacral intercourse was to ensure fertility and prosperity through the coming year. (We can see in this ceremony a continuance of prehistoric peoples' concern for fertility and of their association of fertility with a Mother Goddess.) At the banquet that followed the New Year festival persons representing various elements of the Sumerian culture—summer and winter, farmer and shepherd, copper and iron—debated with one another mockingly, as if to draw all the elements of the culture into its renewal. Sumerian kings overlapped priests, and the kings' identification with Dumuzi made him somewhat divine. Thus persons who prayed to a dead king considered his body a source of blessing, while the live king's basic function was to mediate between the divine realm and the human.

As the king mediated divinity to the political order, so did the temple mediate divinity geographically. The white temple of Urek, for example, was elevated on a terraced platform to dominate the surrounding landscape. Other temples had staired towers (ziggurats) that apparently were symbolic links to heaven. Because the Sumerians seem to have thought their primary reason for being was to serve the gods, they offered sacrifices and libations in the temple each day. A sort of farmer's almanac that has been found advised prayers to a variety of gods, such as Ninkilim, who presided over field mice and vermin, and Ninkasi, who oversaw the production of beer. These were just two of what eventually became the hundreds of gods of the Sumerian pantheon. They were organized into a sort of bureaucracy to reflect the bureaucraces of the temple and the city government. At the top were four chief deities: the rulers of sky, earth, air, and sea. An, the sky god, was the oldest and highest of all the gods, but he was too remote to have much popular effect. Ninhursag, the earth, was a great goddess, a mother from whom issued all living things. Enlil was the god of air and storm and the source of kingly authority. Enki was the god of the waters and also of wisdom. The myths about these gods explained the Sumerian world (and were background for much biblical mythology).

Projecting onto their gods a concern for high moral conduct, the Sumerians developed a fairly extensive written law. For instance, pieces have been found of reform legislation from 2400 B.C.E. that aimed at redressing unjust land annexation and taxation—an effort of the ruler Urukagina to carry out the will of the deity Niagirsu to grant recompense. Thus urbanization was starting to change the archaic religious mentality. Whereas fertility continued to be of great importance, enough institutionalization or culture had developed to make religion also go hand in glove with politics. As people became more conscious of their group identity their religion became more civil and less natural.

Egypt

Prehistoric Egyptians (before 3100 B.C.E.) apparently were a relatively homogeneous people. Ethnically, culturally, and spiritually, they shared a heritage common, old, and optimistic. The land was favoring—warmed by the sun, fertilized by the Nile, protected by the sea and desert from foreign invaders. This sense of tradition and good fortune led to a congenital optimism. According to legend, King Menes united Egypt politically about 3100 B.C.E. That action seems to have been the catalyst Egyptians needed to adopt many of Sumer's achievements (building with brick, constructing boats, writing, using seals). Nevertheless Egypt remained a largely rural culture, a condition that probably preserved it from the neuroses that Sumerian urban life developed. At any rate, Egypt appears to us more self-confident and calm, less anxiety ridden and class conscious. Egyptian children learned from childhood that hard work, virtue, and a little luck could make them a good life. It was possible (as we learn from one early account) for a common laborer to rise to be royal constructor or royal attaché. The fortunate man who gave this account concludes intriguingly, "and I never went to bed angry against anybody." Good fortune with equanimity—that summarizes much of the Egyptian ideal.

Nonetheless, the vaunted stability of Egypt, which maintained itself for over two thousand years, rested on deeper, more explicitly religious foundations. Among the most important were a belief in the consubstantiality of all reality, a belief in divine kingship, and a belief in fulfillment after death. Consubstantiality means the view that all creation, from mice to men, partakes of a single stuff. The world is a sort of giant organism whose energy or vital force all beings participate in. The Egyptians did not speculate about notions like these (their temper was rather practical), but they did intuit or feel them. Thus they felt considerable kinship with animals, as with forces of nature. They also felt considerable kinship with their gods, who were not of a totally different order. By contrast with the Sumerians, they were less craven and self-abasing, for they were not so much the slaves of the gods as lesser participants with them in one integral cosmos—one sacral flow.

Much of this mentality comes out indirectly through diverse, even contradictory, myths. That their myths often contradicted one another does not seem to have bothered the Egyptians at all. Perhaps they sensed that life was so rich or mysterious that all explanations were bound to conflict at some point. Whatever the reason, they found it possible to picture the creation of human beings from the tears of the sun god Re, or from the thoughtful word of Ptah, or by the skill of Khnum, who formed each individual on a potter's wheel and placed him or her in the womb. If one extends this tendency over millennia and adds the need of new capital cities to have their gods dominate the creation account,

Egyptian mythology becomes downright confusing. Consubstantiality was malleable indeed.

Throughout most of Egyptian history the mythology that actually supplied Egypt's cultural and political cement was that of divine kingship. Interpretations of this belief vary, but there seems to be fair agreement that for the popular mind the pharaoh was not so much a god as a manifestation of the divine. In other words, there was no popular doubt that pharaoh was a human being. Equally, however, there was a solid consensus that through pharaoh coursed the sacral order of the cosmos, in such wise that his realm and people received order only through his mediation. Therefore over the many centuries kingship became a marvel of the human species' stability, much like the stability of animal species, which Egyptians found divine because of their constancy from generation to generation.

To clarify the full symbolism of divine kingship in Egypt would take more space than is available in this book, but primarily the divine *maat* ("order" or "law") by which the cosmos ran was passed from heaven to human society through the king. This basic notion gained pregnant connotation in several ways: for instance, by the pharaoh's being regarded as the embodiment of two warring gods, Horus and Seth. By implying both Horus and Seth, pharaoh suggested that they were reconciled in his person. The king also had the title "Son of Re," the sun god. In death he was identified with Osiris, the god who dies and rises. During his legitimate rule pharaoh was the manifestation of Horus, son of Osiris. (Since Seth had wrought the destruction of Osiris and been punished by Horus, the Seth-aspect of pharaoh seems to have been his embracing of whatever threatened life after death, in order to render it innocuous.) Manifoldly, then, the king had ties to the gods.

Some remains of folklore about pharaoh show that the common people probably attached certain magical powers to his person. Thus persons inadvertently brushed by pharaoh's staff are assured they will not die. Similarly those touched by pharaoh's shadow need to have their fears allayed. Should anyone boldly approach too near pharaoh, the serpent adorning his brow would turn into a fire-spitting sorceress. Should pharaoh conceive a plan at night, at dawn it would come into being. This sort of folklore, which does not seem greatly different from that of many other archaic peoples, led one aged ruler to leave his heir some all-too-human advice: Don't let anyone get too close to you. Keep your loneliness and troubles to yourself. If the people see that you are vulnerable, they will reject you, as they have rejected me. (See Frankfort, 1978, pp. 87-88.)

The pharaoh maintained the cosmic connections that allowed him to mediate *maat* in several major ways: a daily greeting of the rising sun, an annual celebration of the New Year, and an elaborate Sed festival thirty years after his enthronement. Because the sun was the most impressive natural phenomenon in the Egyptian orbit, it more than anything else represented ultimate life-power. When the people approached more refined theological views—for instance, during the (somewhat ill-named) monotheistic reform of Akhenaton (1375–1358 B.C.E.)—they tried to make the solar force (in Akhenaton's case, Aton) the sole object of worship. This simplification never took hold, but it indicates where the Egyptians looked spontaneously when they thought of ultimacy and why the rising of the sun each day was a sacral occurrence. The New Year celebration was Egypt's share in the usual archaic effort to integrate human time with divine, cosmic paradigms. The Sed festival usually lasted five days and amounted to a wholesale rehearsal of the multifarious relations between the king and the people, the king and the gods, and the king and the land. The point of this rehearsal was not only to remember or commemorate these relations but also by remembering to reactivate or re-energize them.

As the pyramids demonstrate physically, and texts from many periods show literarily, *death* was never far from the

Egyptian consciousness. Apparently this awareness of mortality did not make the average Egyptian morbid (John Wilson has defended Egypt against such a charge), but it did make providing for death—perhaps more exactly, for afterlife—a societal preoccupation. Moreover, in death as in life the rulers functioned for the whole people. It is well known that the pyramids contained not only preserved corpses (mummies) but also implements, furniture, and the like that the rulers might want in the afterlife. The prevailing notion seems to have been that through death the pharaoh would join the family of gods (to which he already somewhat belonged). His identification with Osiris, god of the under-realm and of vegetative rebirth, did not prevent the rise of mythologies that had him ascend to the heavenly realm of the sun—a fact that simply shows again that conflicting symbolizations did not trouble the Egyptians very much. We know that in later periods the average person fitted his projected destiny to the frame of the ruler's, expecting to descend to the realm of Osiris, undergo a scrutiny and judgment of his worldly life, and then gain a satisfying (if usually vague) continuance of a life like that on earth.

From their concern with death, the Egyptians came to lay stress on preserving the body (though they also had concepts of animating principles akin to a "soul") and on attaining a clear conscience. At the judgment before Osiris a feather would be placed in one pan of a scales; if the deceased's heart carried any guilt heavier than that feather, it would fail the judgment test. Another way to defeat human mortality was to become so filled with *maat* by good attunement to the order of things that *maat's* (divine, and so immortal) substance would make one more powerful than death's destructiveness. *Maat* was difficult to follow—common observation showed that many persons did not lead good lives—but it and the realm of the gods kept strong the notion that there was a higher order of justice that the most profound, desirable humanity intends. Such notions as a higher justice have led scholars to speak of "the dawn of conscience" in Egypt. In the *Book of the Dead*, the Pyramid Texts, and other classical sources, one finds many indications that more than a thousand years before the prophets of the Hebrew Bible, social conscience was sensitive along the Nile.

Osiris and Re

Compared to prehistoric peoples, the Egyptians clarified fertility, death, and order considerably. Because of the blazing sun and the overflowing Nile, they found fertility ready to hand, but it seldom failed to absorb them. The Egyptians regularly represented their divinities in animal form because they were so deeply impressed by the procreative powers of the animals, and they affirmed the prehistoric notion that Sky and Earth were the prime sources of life. The pyramids undoubtedly drew on the same psychic roots as the megaliths, projecting a conquest of death through stone. Egyptian kingship and a conception of cosmic order, however, were significant leaps. Whatever their analogues among prehistoric peoples, in Egypt these ideas gained a precision that made them novel. By concentrating on Osiris, god of the underworld, and Re, god of the sun, we can grasp at least a portion of this novelty.

Osiris and Re had a polar relation such that together they summarized the natural cycle through which *maat* expressed itself. Genealogically Re was a creator god, who made air and moisture "out of himself" (by masturbation). Air and moisture in turn produced earth and sky, which were the source of Osiris. Prior to Osiris, then, all the Egyptian divinities were natural elements. By contrast, Osiris bridged the gap between nature and humanity. Largely for that reason he was associated with pharaoh, who mediated natural *maat* to humanity.

Osiris had several siblings, the most important of whom were Isis (his sister and wife) and Seth (who killed him). Seth represented things that the Egyptians considered foreign and fearful: thunder, the desert, and Asiatics. Isis conceived Horus by Osiris magically—after Seth killed him. This magical event was crucial for the ideology of the pharaoh, since each dead king was assimilated to Osiris and each new successor king was assimilated to Horus. Osiris did not represent only the transitional relation between the old ruler and the new, however; he also represented the fate of the old, deceased pharaoh (and therefore the fate of all Egyptians, who fit pharaoh's mortal pattern). As the son of earth, Osiris descended at death to the under-earth, but as the son also of sky, he would later ascend to heaven. Both his continuance after death under the earth and his later ascension to heaven gave the Egyptians hope for an afterlife. Osiris's ascent to heaven was a lunar symbolism, but because the Egyptians thought of the moon and the sun as twins, Osiris could also move across the sky with the sun god Re for part of the day. Since Re would join the moon (Osiris) under the earth for part of the night, the two gods were together day and night, above earth and below.

Because of his descent to the under-earth and ascent to the sky, Osiris represented all phenomena that waned and waxed. For instance, he stood for the vegetation that "died" in the ground and rose again at the time of new growth. He also stood for the ebb and flow of the Nile and the celestial revolutions of the moon and Orion. In the context of Egyptian agricultural society, identifications such as these made Osiris a very important god.

We see this belief expressed concretely, for instance, in matters concerning grain, an absolute staple of the Egyptian economy. Wheat, barley, and corn virtually determined the Egyptians' prosperity. When they imagined these vital commodities, the Egyptians pictured Osiris: his having been killed and buried in their land made it so fertile in grain. In other words, like the Indonesian myth of Hainuwele, the Egyptian myth of Osiris said that new growing depends on old dying; the decay of Osiris's corpse fertilized the fields of grain.

Indeed, various temples to Osiris had artwork or rituals that represented corn sprouting, while from about 1500 B.C.E. tombs often contained humanoid figures of earth and seeds that were laid on the biers and watered daily until they sprouted. The Egyptians, therefore, drew human death explicitly into the Osiris-process of fertilization and rebirth. As late as the second century of the Christian era, Egyptian peasants planted seed in a mood of mourning.

The annual flooding of the Nile was the condition for Egypt's fertility. Thus rulers would petition the help of the gods and offer libations to try to assure it. Above all, they petitioned Osiris, since he was in the mud or silt that gave the crops their fertility. Though he had been "lost" because of Seth's (the desert's) evil, Osiris was "found" again when the Nile rose in the summer.

Osiris's travel through the heavens was more spiritual than his travel through the cycles of grain or the Nile in that it came to symbolize Egyptian hopes for life after death. If the moon and the stars return each night, bringing a dispassionate splendor, we may hope to return to heavenly splendor after death. Egypt specified this hope for the pharaoh as follows: "I grant thee that thou mayest rise like the sun, rejuvenate thyself like the moon, repeat life like the flood of the Nile." Since cosmic phenomena wax and wane, human beings may wax again after death.

Finally, when we set the Osiris symbolism alongside the other fertility symbolisms we have studied, it shows one peculiarity: the earth to which Osiris descends, under which he rules as god of the dead, is masculine. For other agricultural peoples, as we have seen, the earth was feminine. She was *Mother* Earth, the primordial womb. Why Egypt broke this pattern is hard to determine. Generally speaking, neither Egyptian government nor Egyptian theology stressed the feminine, but that is not unusual. There were a few female rulers, and several significant goddesses, but they were never equal to males. In later periods Isis was Osiris's strong partner, and in early periods the Queen Mother had important functions. Thus Egypt did grant nature's polarity of male and female. When it came to envisioning the earth, however, some predilection for the masculine pushed nature's polarity to the background. That may tell us something about Re, the sun god, who overshadowed even the Earth and the Nile.

Re was but one of several names the sun had throughout most of Egyptian history. The morning sun was Khepri ("self-created"). The evening sun was Atum ("to be at an end"). Generally the creative power of the sun's light and warmth was Re. For Egypt, Re was the most original power in the cosmos.

In one popular creation account Re rises from the primeval waters (chaos) and creates land as a hill on which to stand. In myths and rituals that returned to this creation account, the land of Egypt became the center of the earth, or the local obelisk marked the center of the earth, or the pyramid reproduced Re's original hill. Even pharaoh's throne and sarcophagus were miniatures of the hill of creation. At that original hill, presumably, still pulsated both the divine energy that had overcome chaos, and the strong, central *maat* that had spread out to order all creation. Thus each "in the beginning" brought Re to mind. Every time the Egyptian went to his foundations, he thought of the sun.

The relation between *maat* and Re is interesting: she was both his daughter and his mother. (*Maat* was both personified as a goddess and considered abstractly as an impersonal force.) Insofar as *maat* drew upon the basic creative force, she was an offspring of Re, but insofar as Re followed orderly patterns (for example, when traveling through the sky), he was bound to obey *maat*. Pharaoh needed intimate ties with *maat*, and so Re's regularity made him pharaoh's natural model. When Re's luster inclined the Egyptians to associate him with gold, gold became pharaoh's special ornamentation, "the flesh of the gods," a symbol of immortality. With their animal gods, vegetative cycles, pyramids, and gold, the Egyptians brought the prehistoric themes we studied to the center of the first great civilization.

Greece

In his recent single-volume history of the world, Arnold Toynbee locates the beginnings of Greek civilization in the middle of the third millennium (about 2500 B.C.E.). At that time there arose on the island of Crete what was to be an impressive culture. And though the original stimuli to Cretan culture probably came to the island from Sumeria and Egypt, by 2000 or so it had developed the distinctive form we call Minoan (after Minos, legendary king of Crete). Minoan culture produced a linear script, then had a new efflorescence around 1580–1450 B.C.E., when the first true Greeks, then called Minyans, began to interact with the Cretan natives. These Greeks were Aryan-speaking Indo-Europeans (of the same general stock as Aryan Indians and Iranians). Later known as Mycenaeans or Achaeans, they established a capital city at Cnossus and presided over a golden cultural age from about 1400 to 1150. After 1100 B.C.E. invaders called Dorians overran Crete and threw it into a dark age (literacy even passed from the Cretan scene). Nonetheless, memories of the original golden age haunted the classical age of Athens, and sensitive interpreters such as Plato knew that Greek culture had roots beyond Homer in a glorious early time. To show the origins Greek religion had in hunting and agriculture, let us first survey the Goddess cult that excavations on Crete have revealed.

From neolithic times people on Crete used the island's caves as cultural centers. They lived in caves, buried their dead in caves, and performed rites to the Goddess in caves. This early use of caves remained influential in the form of the labyrinth that fascinated later Greeks. We know from our study of miners that the Goddess's womb was a sort of archetype. That seems to have been true in Greece: the

Cretan cave beginnings remained lively in the Greek psyche. Specifically, at the origins of Greek religion lies a fertility figure, or mistress of the animals, from prehistoric hunting times.

The excavations of the Cretan caves have yielded statuettes of this fertility figure and other artifacts that tie her to burials or changes-of-state. For instance, archaeologists have found numerous representations of butterflies and bees (animals with marked metamorphoses). They have also found remains of bull horns, double axes, trees, animals, cosmic pillars, and blood sacrifices. As a whole these remains suggest a complex, several-layered religious activity centered on life—fertility and immortality.

Some of the life-associations of the Cretan artifacts probably go back many millennia before Minoan-Mycenaean culture. In nearby Anatolia (modern Turkey) excavations from sanctuaries in Catal Huyuk show that around 7000 B.C.E. worship involved offering skulls and various gifts (jewels, textiles, weapons) to a female deity in the three aspects of young woman, mother, and crone. Figurines represent this deity giving birth, her cave sites are adorned with breasts or womblike symbols, and she is often set in the midst of animals, especially bulls or leopards. The double axe, symbol of the storm god, represents the archaic conviction that stormy rain fecundates Mother Earth. Last, excavators have found many figurines of a slight male god, a boy or youth who most likely is the Goddess's child or lover. Clearly, the dominant female of Catal Huyuk is a fertility goddess. (See Eliade, 1978*a*, p. 46.)

Many of these themes were lost or pushed into the background when the religion of Zeus and the Olympians emerged to dominate Greece. That religion derived from the Indo-European portion of the Greek stock, and like other species of Indo-European religion (portions of Hinduism, for instance), it stressed the phenomena of the sky rather than those of the earth. The dark age brought by the Dorians makes conjectural how the shift from the Great Goddess to Zeus occurred, but the greatest likelihood is that immigrant peoples brought with them their Aryan legends, which slowly evolved into the mythology of the Olympians. The older Goddess religion persisted but in changed shape. Thus later myths about Demeter and Persephone maintained the notion of a fertile maternal source of life, while Hera, Artemis, and Aphrodite all bore features that set them in the general frame of the fertility Goddess. In the Eleusinian mysteries, which were a major counterbalance to the sky-oriented religion of Zeus, Demeter's search for Persephone in the underworld had overtones of an agricultural deity's descent into the bowels of the earth (for instance, Osiris's descent). It seems clear, then, that Greek religion never replaced the Goddess. For all that Zeus and the Olympians represented a victory for the sky—and so perhaps a victory for the "upward" movement of mind and intellectual light—the Greek concern for fertility, vitality, and immortality maintained a hardy interest in the earth and the Mother.

Dionysius and Apollo

Like the Egyptians, the Greeks tended to provide for nature's polarities by overlapping symbolisms or mythologies. It is not atypical, then, that a god like Dionysius represented fertility and vegetative growth as much as the Mother Goddess did. He also represented life's irrational side, the realm of emotion or passion. Paired with Apollo, who represented control and reason, Dionysius symbolized Greece's clarification of human nature, which took it to the verge of breaking with archaic trends by stressing the uniqueness of human rationality and freedom.

Dionysius was an eccentric among the classical Greek gods—not really an Olympian. Mythologically he was the son of Zeus, but by a mortal woman. Historically his cult came to Greece from northern lands and always remained somewhat foreign. Emotionally many feared his cult because of the frenzy to which it could lead. By the time Greece was on the verge of discovering mind (Snell's famous study reminds us that mind did indeed have to be discovered), such frenzy seemed a step backward toward barbarism or primitivism. As we see in Euripides' play *The Bacchae,* followers of Dionysius danced and drank themselves into a state of wild enthusiasm. They considered Dionysius the vital divinity of the grape, vegetation, and wild animals. In *The Bacchae,* the maenads (women followers of Dionysius) culminated their mountain revels by tearing wild animals apart and eating their flesh raw so as to commune with the divinity of animal life. That is strong stuff indeed.

Clearly, then, Dionysius symbolized powerful life-forces. E. R. Dodds has also associated him with "the blessings of madness." To go out of oneself ecstatically has always been a powerful religious option, and devotees of Dionysius embraced the practice vigorously. They saw their god as an entryway to the total life-force, a god who brought in his train water and germination, blood and sperm, and animal epiphanies as a bull, a lion, or a goat. In the joy of his dance, Dionysius made vitality itself an ecstatic experience.

By contrast, Apollo was an Olympian god, concerned with law and order. In time he came to symbolize many of classical Greece's highest virtues: serenity, harmony, balance, and order. Through his oracle at Delphi, Apollo gave counsel on matters of liturgical propriety and ritual purification. For example, one Greek custom was that homicides had to purify themselves from pollution, and Apollo presided over this purification.

The pythia, or oracular priestess of the shrine at Delphi, would utter strange sayings while in a trance, as though her function went back to archaic shamanism. But the Delphic oracle that became most famous—probably because it best represented Apollonian wisdom—was "Know thyself." In germ that saying endorsed philosophy, science, art, and music, for all of which Apollo was patron. Self-knowledge therefore took the Greek mind in a direction quite different from Dionysian irrationality. Indeed, it took the Greek mind to a deification of thought and spirit.

The fact that Apollo and Dionysius shared the shrine at Delphi (Apollo vacating it annually so that Dionysius could hold sway) clearly shows the balance in which the Greeks set these two gods. Each god complemented the other; both were needed for a whole human psyche. As the sky gods did not oust the earth goddesses, so the god of law did not oust the god of spontaneity. By its both/andness, Greece retained archaic religion while advancing to the threshold of an experience that also broke it. That experience was philosophy, in which the consubstantiality of the natural world cracked, because of the pressures of transcendence (a reality beyond the natural world). Since transcendence appears more clearly in the world religions, however, let us summarize the archaic religious mind of the early civilizations in terms of what Eric Voegelin has called "the cosmological myth."

The Cosmological Myth

By their density and duration the populations of Sumeria, Egypt, and Greece considerably advanced the prehistoric themes we studied in the first chapter. As we have taken pains to show, much in these civilizations depended on prehistoric themes, and much kept continuity with them. Clearly, however, there were also advances or new departures. If fertility can represent the old themes, then conscience and mind can represent the new departures. Egypt sharpened conscience by myths of judgment after death. Greece sponsored mind first by revering Apollo and then by developing natural philosophy.

Both conscience and mind have an energy to go beyond the natural world. For example, conscience can search the natural and human worlds for justice, find that it never fully occurs, and therefore project justice to a "no place" (a utopia)—a courtroom under the earth, where souls are tried after death, or a heavenly realm, where a power more than natural or human rewards the good and punishes the wicked. Similarly, mind can continue to probe the intelligibility of nature or human society, turning even to examine its own spiritual structure, until one day it realizes that it is moved in its depths by nothing less than "God," a holy reality quite different from either nature or humanity.

A major thesis of Eric Voegelin's magnificent *Order and History* is that the Greek philosophers Plato and Aristotle approached this realization of God's movement in the depths of the human spirit, thereby verging on breaking the cosmological myth. The cosmological myth is a storied explanation of reality that emphasizes the consubstantiality of all creatures. Symbolically it says that all creation participates in a single "stuff." Thus there is no break between rocks and plants, plants and animals, animals and human beings, human beings and gods; all merely represent different points or stages in a continuum. The ultimate reality of a god is holy, but so too is the ultimate reality of a rock, because the world—the ordered whole we call a cosmos—is a single living system. The exchanges that occur within the cosmos, its transformations of energy and transactions of power, form a closed economy. Since no reality exists outside the cosmos (it ranges from the stars to the depths of the sea), all reality moves to one pulsation or spin. The seasons, night and day, biological clocks, male and female—all color one cosmological rhythm. Nothing is conceivable outside the cosmos. Nature's hold is absolute.

The cosmological myth was implicit in prehistoric world-views, but it was undeveloped. In civilizational societies it emerged with considerable clarity. Sacral kingship, for instance, was a primary expression of it: a civilizational culture received the orderly flow of the one cosmic power through the king who stood at the peak of its society. That the king stay in harmony with the flow of nature (*maat*) was therefore crucial. The ceremonies of coronation and the New

Year and other festivals aimed at just this effect. Ancient Egypt is a fine example of a society in the cosmological style, but so too are ancient China, ancient India, and ancient Persia. Even Greece moved in this pattern, insofar as its popular culture never broke the close ties to nature that both the Olympian deities and the under-earth deities entailed.

For Voegelin only classical philsophy and Israelite revelation broke the cosmological myth effectively. Only in those two cultural instances was the total adequacy of the natural world split. Through the rift appeared what further development would make the doctrine of creation from nothingness, with its corollaries that divinity transcends the world and nature is contingent.

At this point we have reached a definition—a boundary that separates the archaic from the postarchaic. Prehistoric religion and the religions of the early civilizational societies lived, moved, and had their being in the orbit of nature. The glimpses they had of a nature-transcending God were not strong enough to overturn the evidence that the cosmos was an encompassing parent. By contrast, the "leaps in being" (Voegelin's phrase) that occurred in the creative burst of the axial period of human history distanced humanity from nature. Karl Jaspers has used the term "axial period" to designate the time around 500 B.C.E. when the great thinkers who still influence our lives flourished. They include Plato, Aristotle, Confucius, Lao Tzu, the Buddha, the writers of the Upanishads, the Hebrew prophets, Zoroaster, the Mahavira, and others. These thinkers commonly intuited that the human spirit steps out of nature. They did not develop this insight fully, nor did they all develop it in the same way, but they all felt it in germ. That germ begot the postarchaic world-views. As we shall see, the postarchaic world-views never left the cosmological myth completely behind, but merely by recognizing it as a myth, they broke its inevitability and launched a new era.

Bibliography

Barraclough, Geoffrey, ed. *The Times Atlas of World History.* Maplewood: Hammond, 1979.

Bleeker, C. J. *"The Religion of Ancient Egypt." In Historia Religionum, I: Religions of the Past,* C. Jouco Bleeker and George Widengren, eds. Leiden: E. J. Brill, 1969, pp. 40-113.

Brandon, S. G. F. *Religion in Ancient History.* New York: Charles Scribner's Sons, 1969.

Dietrich, B. C. *The Origins of Greek Religion.* New York: Walter de Gruyter, 1974.

Dodds, E. R. *The Greeks and the Irrational.* Berkeley: University of California Press, 1966.

Eliade, Mircea. *A History of Religious Ideas, I: From the Stone Age to the Eleusinian Mysteries.* Chicago: University of Chicago Press, 1978.

Evans, Arthur. *The Earlier Religion of Greece in the Light of Cretan Discoveries.* London: Macmillan, 1931.

Frankfort, Henri. *Before Philsosphy.* Baltimore, Penguin, 1946.

———. *Kingship and the Gods.* Chicago: University of Chicago Press, 1978.

Gimbutas, Marija. "Old Europe, C. 7000–3000 B.C.," *Journal of Indo-European Studies, I* (1973), 1-20.

Hammond, Mason. *The City of the Ancient World.* Cambridge: Harvard University Press, 1972.

Jaspers, Karl. *The Origin and Goal of History.* New Haven: Yale University Press, 1953.

Kenyon, Kathleen M. *Digging Up Jericho.* New York: Praeger, 1957.

Kramer, Samuel Noah. *The Sumerians.* Chicago, University of Chicago Press, 1963.

Landes, G. M. "Jericho." In *The Interpreter's Dictionary of the Bible, Supplementary Volume,* pp. 472-73. Nashville: Abingdon Press, 1976.

Mumford, Lewis. *The City in History.* New York: Harcourt, Brace, & World, 1961.

Parrot, Andre. *Sumer.* London: Thames & Hudson, 1960.

Pritchard, James. B., ed. *Ancient Near Eastern Texts.* 3d ed. Princeton: Princeton University Press, 1969.

Ringgren, Helmer. *Religions of the Ancient Near East.* Philadelphia: Westminster, 1973.

Snell, Bruno. *The Discovery of Mind.* New York: Harper & Row, 1960.

Toynbee, Arnold. *Mankind and Mother Earth.* Oxford: Oxford University Press, 1976.

Voegelin, Eric. *Order and History.* 4 vols. Baton Rouge: Louisiana State University Press, 1956-74.

Wilson, John A. *The Burden of Egypt.* Chicago: University of Chicago Press, 1951.

Chapter 3:
Archaism in the World Religions

Thus far we have traced dominant archaic themes (closeness to nature, reverence for fertility, and concern with world-influencing spirits) through prehistoric religion and then summarized civilizational religion in terms of the cosmological myth. In this chapter we extend our study of archaic themes and the cosmological myth in the world religions.

The term *world religions* is not very precise. Roughly it means the religions that have flowered into a full system and spread to several cultures. The best examples are Buddhism, Christianity, and Islam, but other candidates also deserve mention. For example, Hinduism certainly developed a full system of scriptures, myths, rituals, philosophical reflections, and social norms, and it moved outside the Indian subcontinent to influence Southeast Asia and Indonesia. Similarly, Confucianism inspired a full system of philosophy and rites that formed the ethical consciousness not just of China but of all East Asia. Taoism was more aesthetic and diffuse, but it too spread out beyond strictly Chinese culture. Finally, we could also call Judaism a world religion, since it both developed a rich system and had devotees in many different lands.

Nonetheless, the clearest instances of truly world religious systems are Buddhism, Christianity, and Islam, and so they best serve our limited purposes. Not only do they influence more than a third of all persons living today, they have also inspired some of humanity's richest cultural history. The archaic elements that we find in these three religions therefore make the basic case that archaism took no holiday in the great systems. Hindu fertility interest in the *lingam* and *yoni* (symbols of male and female organs), Confucian sacrifice and ancestor veneration (see Yang, pp. 253-57), Taoist love of living nature, and Jewish folklore about dybbuks and the evil eye could easily demonstrate that the other world religions stayed significantly archaic.

Buddhism

Buddhism exists because the Nepalese prince Gautama (ca. 563–483 B.C.E.) came to enlightenment (*Buddha* means "the enlightened one"). Let us therefore begin by considering Gautama's enlightenment. After a first encounter with old age, sickness, and death (the somewhat mythical sources tell us), the prince decided to leave his pampered life and solve the problem of imperfect human existence. His first recourse was asceticism and yogic meditation. The northern India of his time was full of ascetics and meditation masters (the Mahavira, founder of Jainism, was but a generation older than Gautama, while some of the *rishis*, or seers, who produced the Upanishads were contemporaries), so it was not difficult to obtain teachers. But these teachers failed to give Gautama full peace. Only when he resolutely vowed to remain at his meditation spot until he gained saving knowledge did he win through to *bodhi*: the direct perception of reality that cut the knots of ignorance and loosed him from *samsara* (the world of rebirth).

The traditional accounts of Gautama's passage to enlightenment told of three stages. Sitting in meditation, the Buddha-to-be passed to the highest form of trance, whence he made three progressive leaps in understanding. First, he saw each of his previous existences. This knowledge (or the later interpretation of Buddha's experience) depended on the

Indian cultural assumption of reincarnation. Depending on the quality of one's previous existence (*karma*), one was now well or poorly poised to gain liberation (*moksha* or *nirvana*). Reincarnation has not been limited to India, however. In their interesting interpretation of Gautama's enlightenment, Robinson and Johnson (pp. 29-30) note that many shamans have claimed to know their previous lives. In terms Huston Smith recently has coined, such knowledge pertains to the "intermediate plane," the realm of psychic phenomena that many cultures have affirmed. (See Smith, pp. 38-48.)

In his second leap in understanding, Gautama surveyed living beings everywhere and saw that their dying and being reborn was a function of their karmic state. For Robinson and Johnson this too is a shamanic power found outside Buddhist or Indian culture. It is, in their own words, "widely attested in archaic cultures" (p. 30). Buddha gave this insight his own twist by linking births and actions together in an ethical equation (good deeds beget good births, bad deeds beget bad births), but the power itself might be implicit in full access to the intermediate plane.

The third leap in understanding brought the distinctively Buddhist breakthrough: the four noble truths. Gautama saw that (1) human existence is radically painful; (2) the cause of this pain is desire, buttressed by ignorance; (3) if one stops desire—by an existential insight that removes ignorance—one will stop life's radical pain; and (4) the way to stop desire is to embark on the noble eightfold path of right views, right intentions, right speech, right conduct, right livelihood, right effort, right mindfulness, and right concentration. (See Conze, pp. 186-87.)

By one defensible interpretation, then, two-thirds of Buddha's enlightenment was a personal appropriation of archaic insights. Where Buddha broke with the mytho-symbolic mentality that characterized prehistoric and early civilizational wisdoms was in penetrating the structure of existence analytically. This penetration depended on generations of yogic

Indian forebears. From prehistoric times India had fostered experimentalists who worked with human interiority, human spirituality. Just as Mircea Eliade has epitomized shamanism as archaic techniques of ecstasy, so Eliade has epitomized yoga as the means of attaining *enstasis* ("autonomy," "dispassionate self-control"). Enstasis seems to break with the archaic world-view and the cosmological myth because it sets spirit over against matter; however, in most cases, including the Buddha and Patanjali (the classical Hindu theoretician of yoga), the break was certainly incomplete.

For the Buddha himself, as best we can recapture his world-view, enlightenment did not remove either the gods (beings of impressive powers who yet remained in the realm of samsara) or the personification of evil, Mara. John Bowker (pp. 269-84) has shown the canonical basis for concluding that Buddha, far from being atheistic, retained the polytheistic world-view of his Hindu contemporaries. Further, according to both the *Buddhacarita* of Ashvaghosa (the most noted traditional biography of the Buddha) and the Jataka tales (the collection of popular lore), on the way to enlightenment Buddha had to defeat Mara and his three daughters (Discontent, Delight, and Thirst). (See Conze, pp 48-49; Warren, pp. 76-82.) It may be that Gautama's own sense of the spirit-world was less vivid than that which later Buddhist tradition attributed to him. Nonetheless, he probably did not break cleanly with the intermediate plane, because the canonical as well as the popular Buddhist tradition remained immersed in it.

As the *Buddhacarita* reports, the Buddha's birth had numerous mythomagical aspects. His mother Maya had a dream of a kingly white elephant entering her body. She conceived, and the child issued from her side without causing her pain or injury. He shone with auspicious marks, took seven steps, and announced: "For enlightenment was I born, for the good of all that lives. This is the last time that I have been born into this world of becoming" (Conze, p. 36).

Similarly, at the Buddha's death, when he entered nirvana, the earth quaked, fire fell from the sky, violent winds raged, and the moon waned. (Conze, p. 63) Whatever the transcendence enlightenment had brought, Buddha's followers did not understand it to mean a radical break with nature. The natural portents at Buddha's death, like the spiritual portents at his birth, placed enlightenment-being within the cosmic circuit.

For reasons such as these, Voegelin judges that the Buddha, like the Upanishads and Chinese speculation, did not break the cosmological myth and differentiate a fully postarchaic world-view. (See Voegelin, pp. 328-29, 319-23, 285-87.) If we move now to later Buddhist tradition, we see this judgment expressly verified. For example, a later tale of the Buddha says that after his enlightenment he showed off his miraculous powers to impress his relatives. Rising in the air, he cut his body into pieces, let his head and limbs fall, and them reassembled himself. Some analysts see this tale as a basis for Indian fakirism and for the famous Indian rope-trick. (See Eliade, 1964, pp. 428-30.) The Jataka tales are a lush garden of magical transformations through which the Buddha becomes a fairy, a sprite, a marsh-crow, a peacock, a quail, a lion, and other animals in order to teach a lesson or save a soul. Not only do these tales concretize the canonical doctrine of *upaya* (the "skill in means" to save souls that the Buddha has) so that the masses can grasp it, they also reveal how the ordinary Buddhist's world remained compact: a melding of spirit and matter, imagination and intellect, myth and philosophy, animals and gods. Such compactness is typically archaic. Nature, fertility, and world-influencing spirits weave back and forth and focus myths and rituals because demons, animals, humans, and gods all swarm together; all are more consubstantial than disparate.

When Buddhism emigrated from India (it began to decline there from the seventh century C.E.), its magical sense of the Buddha and its archaic world-view went with it. Thus Chinese literature of the sixteenth century, as represented by the famous novel *Monkey*, shows a popular religion in which the Buddhist strain believes that the soul of one person can be put into the body of another, that money burned in this world can be deposited to an ancestor's account in the next, and that Bodhisattvas (Buddhas-to-be) such as Kuan-yin can move holy persons to such good effects as finding a scriptural text. (See Waley, pp. 110-18.) Japanese funeral customs, which were heavily influenced by Buddhist beliefs, developed a full ceremonial. Commenting on it Earhart says: "A good deal of superstition prevailed as to lucky or unlucky days for cremation and interment, and geomancers were often employed to choose a propitious time" (p 63). Geomancers are diviners who specialize in natural earth patterns. Obviously such patterns depend on the cosmological myth for their influence on human religion.

Both Chinese and Japanese Buddhism tended to follow Mahayana ("great vehicle") schools. Such schools not only favored speculative developments in philosophy and worked spiritual accommodations for the laity (so that Buddhism could serve more than monks); they also developed naturalistic rituals and ceremonies. For instance, Zen Buddhism, which belongs to the Mahayana family, interwove with Japanese aesthetics to inspire the tea ceremony, flower arrangement, swordsmanship and the martial arts. In these elegant cultural developments, as in such elegant poetry as the haiku, one sees the cosmological myth at its most refined. The haiku of a master like Basho (seventeenth century) point the oneness of all reality to the arresting movement of a bird, the graceful fall of a blossom. Similarly, the famous Zen rock garden of Kyoto conveys graphically how nature and spirit are a single field. Like the bare raked sand in which the angular rocks sit, nature and spirit are an "emptiness." Enlightenment means being so struck by an angular creature that one drops dualistic thinking and sees the consubstantiality of the whole.

Vajrayana, a Buddhist family that developed after Mahayana, flowered most fully in Tibet. It put Mahayana dicta about the oneness of all reality, the unity of *samsara* (the illusory world of rebirth) and *nirvana* (the real world of enlightened spirit), into elaborate ceremonial form. Tibetan Buddhism retained a strong influence from its native shamanic tradition (*Bon* religion), which was fascinated with the gravitation of libidinal energies toward sex and death. *Tantra* was the name of a parallel fascination India had developed. In both Hinduism and Buddhism, *tantra* encouraged the use of mantras (magical sounds), mandalas (magical shapes), and rites that broke with standard morality. For instance, tantrists might eat forbidden foods (meat, blood), drink forbidden alcohol, and engage in forbidden sexual activities (simulated or real). Whether in India or Tibet, the Buddhist reason for such practices was to assault what society took to be real and moral. In obedience to a guru the tantrist set out to throw off ordinary reality. Ordinary reality was a trap, a beguilement. Therefore those who sought enlightenment and nirvana had to escape this trap; the disciplined use of primal energies, which mandalas, mantras, and sexual rites could tap, helped them. Insofar as they were focused on the energy of nature or fertility, the tantrists worked in an archaic mode.

The third Buddhist family, the Theravada, claimed to be most faithful to the original traditions. Theravada was slower than Mahayana to accommodate the laity, and slower than Vajrayana to encourage *tantra*. Nonetheless, Theravada affirmed ghosts, demons, three hells, and three heavens. (See Robinson and Johnson, pp. 34-38.) In Thailand today one can see the full color of a Theravadian imagination. Several *wats* (shrines) in the Imperial Palace Compound are guarded by twelve-foot statues of warrior spirits. In modern Burma anthropologists have found Buddhism very tolerant toward a lively cult of household and village spirits (*nats*). Typically a *nat* dislikes birth, death, sex, and fire, and so when any of these occurs a devout Buddhist will remove the coconut that represents the *nat*, lest it observe and take offense. When naming a child, celebrating a wedding, or traversing a field, one must also provide for the *nats*. Women say they must treat the *nats* like husbands: care for them, defer to them, and not injure their pride.

Christianity

Buddhism runs a gamut of mentalities, from deeply critical to wildly animistic. No scholar would say that Buddhism did not advance beyond prehistoric or early civilizational archaism; on the other hand, no scholar would deny that many archaic ingredients continued. It is the same with Christianity. Building on Jewish achievements, Jesus and the Christian masters developed a religion centered on a world-transcendent God. Nonetheless, neither Jesus nor the masters (let alone the mass of ordinary Christians) left archaic themes completely behind.

First, considerable archaism existed in the Jewish tradition that Jesus inherited. Although the Hebrew Bible established one God as the creator of the world, it did not completely clear the field of archaic questions. For instance, Genesis did not make God create the world from *nothing*. Some Israelite theologians intuited the farthest reaches of transcendence, where God is utterly free of everything finite. We see their work in the interpretation of Abraham's religious experience (Genesis 14 and 15), Moses' religious experience (Exodus 14), the prophetic experience of Second Isaiah, and the experience of Wisdom (Proverbs 1–9, Job 28). Still, the bulk of the Hebrew Bible blurred the transcendence of a *creator ex nihilo* by anthropomorphic or mythic portrayals of divine action in time. Moreover, Israel's stress on God's self-revelation through history did not negate the divine presence in the cycles of nature. Indeed, the history of revelation, as Voegelin's analysis (pp. 59-113) of "historiogenesis" shows, was significantly mythic and stylized, while the prophets had to fight priests, kings, and people who wanted a fertility cult. Job speaks of Satan and of God's majesty in nature, while the

Jewish apocalyptic literature at the end of the biblical period made mythical beasts serve bitter hopes for vindication.

Second, Jesus appropriated this biblical inheritance and reworked it. He appropriated the transcendence of the God of the covenant, confessing with Israel's *shema* that the Lord his God was one. Jesus' first command was to love this God with the whole mind, heart, soul, and strength. His second command was to love one's neighbor as oneself. In putting his own touch on these two Jewish precepts, Jesus spoke of God as an intimate parent and of his neighbor as any fellow human being in need. These radical interpretations made him a powerful charismatic figure, a *hasid* of special eloquence. (See Vermes, pp. 223-25.) More problematic for his contemporaries was Jesus' free interpretation of traditional religious law: Sabbath obligations, dietary customs, and restrictions about contact with "unclean" persons. In making these interpretations that stressed human welfare and forgiveness, Jesus ran afoul of the religious establishment. Since the legal mentality of that establishment was a development beyond most archaism, Jesus' further development was doubly postarchaic.

More archaic, though, were Jesus' apparent beliefs about demons, spirits, and angels. Here two hermeneutical issues must be dispatched. First, I acknowledge that all the New Testament data we have on Jesus' beliefs were liable to the influence of the theologizing of at least a generation of Jesus's followers. Second, the implication of Jesus's apparent belief in demons for our current wariness in accrediting demons can remain moot. (In other words, an archaic belief such as this may or may not be more true than a modern critical judgment that demons, spirits, and angels are psychic projections. Similar issues arise with Muhammad, whose visions of angels the modern mind is equally slow to accredit.) Without prejudice we simply note that in casting out devils Jesus stands in continuity with exorcists and healers of archaic traditions the world over. (Jesus's cures are less germane than his exorcisms. Most of them merely remind us that body and spirit conjoin in all human sickness or health, and that a living creator surely can operate on us creatures. The medical records of Lourdes are more impressive than doctrinaire atheism.)

Joachim Jeremias's study of Jesus's own proclamation has a chapter (pp. 85-96) that deals with the theme of overcoming the rule of Satan. First, the stories of Jesus's miracles frequently subserve this theme: Jesus, possessed of a greater power than the devil, is loosing bodies and spirits from the devil's dominion. (See Acts 10:38) After all due provision for the tendency of the early community to embelish Jesus's figure with miraculous powers, Jeremias finds a historical nucleus to these stories: Jesus performed healings that astonished his contemporaries. Second, the Gospels portray mental illness as possession by demons. Jesus sharpens this contemporary theory by linking the appearance of demons to Satan, their commander (Luke 10:19, Mark 5:9, Matthew 10:25). The Gospel of Mark especially shows Jesus's exorcisms as battles with Satan. These struggles are convincing signs that the kingdom of God, the definitive time of salvation, has dawned in Jesus's person. As Edward Schillebeeckx makes clear, Jesus's central significance has always been the salvation— healing, fulfillment—that Christians have found in him. (See pp. 19-23.)

Apparently Jesus found an important proof of his mission in his power to contest evil successfully—physical and spiritual evil alike. To liberate human beings from disease, hatred, injustice, and hopelessness (and do it in dramatic, bodily fashion) was to tear down the regime of Satan, the *exthros* or "disrupter of creation." The testimony of the Gospels on this point is so solid that to make it purely the creation of the post-Easter community would destroy all use of the writings as historical sources. There is every likelihood, then, that Jesus set part of the import of the Kingdom in the intermediate plane, and that he had a lively, archaic sense of the reality of spirits. Morton Kelsey has recently made psychological translations that bridge the distance from our assumptions to Jesus's archaism and make his spirits more credible today. (See pp. 51-85.)

Fertility and intimacy with nature do not figure prominently in Jesus's message, nor does immersion in the cosmological myth. Jesus loved the natural world about him (the lilies of the field), and likened spiritual growth to natural processes (the seed falling in the ground), but he was too concerned with social problems, and with the end of history that the Kingdom implied, to be captivated by these other archaic themes. Some stimulus existed for early Christianity to associate Jesus with the dying and rising gods (Osiris prominently among them) that had come into the Hellenistic milieu, but the first understanding of Jesus's resurrection was more eschatological than archaic—that is, the early theologians saw the resurrection as an act of God that brought the end-time of human fulfillment into the disciples' experience. (On the complex Jewish background, see Schillebeeckx, pp. 516 ff.) Later the church capitalized on Easter's spring date, associating it with nature's rebirth, just as it set Christmas at the winter solstice to heighten the appearance of the "sun of justice" in the midst of darkness. None of this liturgical Christology set Jesus back in the cosmological myth, however.

The Christian masters, beginning with the apostle Paul, retained an archaic sense of evil and world-influencing spirits. Ephesians 2:2 speaks of a pre-Christian life as "following the prince of the power of the air, the spirit that is now at work in the sons of disobedience." The same book says in 6:12 "For we are not contending against flesh and blood, but against the principalities, against the powers, against the world rulers of this present darkness, against the spiritual hosts of wickedness in the heavenly places." Other Pauline Epistles repeat these themes. Augustine and Aquinas took over such scripture, commenting, for instance, that Christ allowed himself to be tempted by the devil to give us an example of resistance (*De*

Trin., 4; *Summa Theologic*, III, q. 41, a.1). Luther and Calvin also continued to speak of being freed from the devil's bondage (*Preface to Romans; Institutes*, 4:1). In these masters, as in the developing theology of each major Christian branch (Roman, Orthodox, and Protestant), reliance on scripture meant accepting the reality of devils and angels, hell and heaven.

Just as Christianity informed European culture, so Christian rites, saints, and sacramentals focused the archaic imaginations of peasant peoples. The rite for baptism included an exorcism of Satan. The lore on saints took up folk beliefs in tutelary spirits. For example, Saint Blaise offered protection against sore throats, and Saint Patrick freed Ireland of snakes. The sacramentals—medals, holy water— functioned like amulets for many simple faithful; up to recent times medals of Saint Christopher protected travelers on their journeys, and holy water kept the devil away. In Orthodox lands holy icons, especially those of Christ's mother, Mary, were a source of blessing, as were the graves of wonder-workers. Protestantism stripped away ritual, veneration of the saints, sacramentals, and icons, but it still spoke of the devil and witches. Also, simple Protestants often used the Bible for divination; opening the sacred text at random, they took as divine counsel the first passage they saw.

Mircea Eliade (1976) has shown parallels between European witchcraft and the shamanism and magic of other cultural areas. In its obsession with witches, Christian Europe of the fifteenth to eighteenth centuries put great numbers of persons to death, perhaps as many as nine million (Daly, p. 183). Most of these were women, whom orthodox doctrine held more vulnerable than men to Satan's sway. Thus the priests who wrote the *Malleus Maleficarum,* a catechism of demonology that appeared in 1486, said flatly that "all witchcraft comes from carnal lust which is in women insatiable." The Inquisition assumed that heresy dovetailed with Satanism, an attitude that perhaps made burning heretics at the stake more palatable. The most notorious witch hunts in the United States occurred at Salem, Massachusetts, in the seventeenth century. They brought death to twenty accused witches: thirteen women and seven men. (Rhode Island officially eliminated hanging for convicted witches in 1768.)

In the case of European witchcraft, biblical references to the devil joined with pre-Christian notions of consorting with evil spirits to tap fears both ancient and deep. Other, parallel ways also showed that the new faith was but a veneer over old, indeed archaic, pagan religion. At the beginning of the twentieth century, Rumanian peasants had customs that went back to Homeric Greece. (Eliade, 1970, p. vii) Such customs joined the Christian faith to the concern of agriculturalists for fertility, begetting blessings for the fields, harvest festivals, and the like. Among maritime peoples the results were analogous: blessings for the annual run of the herring, prayers for the sailors' safety, homage to the patron saint of the fleet. Midwifery, alchemy, and blacksmithing sometimes grafted archaic fascination with herbs and metals onto Christian culture; at other times they operated secretly within Christian culture. Germanic and Celtic peasants retained their fairies and woodsprites, and Scandanavian Christianity never fully routed many pre-Christian customs and gods.

Thus the faith of Europe, the Christian heartland, retained myriad archaic features. All the more, then, did the faith of colonized lands such as Central America, Africa, and Haiti. Maude Oakes's anthropological study, *The Two Crosses of Todos Santos,* explores a fine example of Christianity's syncretic fusion with a native religion of Central America. The Mam Indians of Guatemala, whom she studied from 1945 to 1947, practiced many of the old Mayan ways, though Christianity had long been the official faith. A brief paragraph gives the flavor of this syncretism: "One day, when Simona, my servant for a time, and I were having lunch, the church bells tolled. A few seconds later a wasp flew into the room, and Simona said, 'It is the spirit of the dead.' Then, after a few minutes, she exclaimed, 'Senorita, when someone dies in a family, they eat little that day.' 'What do they eat?' I asked. 'Just *tortillas* and a cup of blood.' 'Blood of a cooked animal or of a freshly killed one?' 'Blood of a freshly killed one, an animal killed that very day,' she answered'' (p. 44).

A similar syncretism appears in Voudoun, the religion of the vast majority of Haitians. Maya Deren has described it in the case of one Haitian man: "Titon . . . had refused to abandon the ancestral loa [Voudoun gods], although, like all other Voudoun serviteurs [devotees], he sincerely insisted that he believed in the Christian God and in Jesus, and always made ritual obeisance to these before passing on to the Voudoun service. As a matter of fact, he knew the Catholic litanies so well that he was often called upon to assist the houngan [Voudoun priest] by standing in as the *pret-savanne*, or bush priest, whose function it is to invoke the benediction of the Christian deity upon the Voudoun ceremony to follow'' (p. 54). There is a complex African background to Haitian Voudoun, because of the many tribes that were carried off from Africa to Haiti by putative Christians. In summary, though, Voudoun's many gods, concept of the human soul, spirit possession, and healing ceremonies all manifest a vivid archaic sense of world-influencing spirits.

So, whether in Europe, Latin America, Africa, or Haiti, the message is that native archaic religion has died hard. Historically only the educated upper classes have appropriated a thoroughly Christian world-view stressing monotheism, creation from nothingness, and Christ's subjugation of all evil spirits. The uneducated masses have continued to work the fields or sail the seas with reverence for archaic forces. In recent centuries mass education has changed this situation, as has the secularizing influence of technology, though actually they both raise the question whether Christianity can survive the blows to mystery that modernity implies. Mystery is not strictly an archaic concept, but the concrete religious appreciation of it (God as a fullness beyond human comprehension) so often engages archaic instincts that the complete demise of archaism may de facto entail the demise of most mystagogy.

Islam

Just as Buddhism is the religion generated by Gautama's enlightenment and Christianity is the religion generated by Jesus's salvation, so Islam is the religion generated by Muhammad's prophecy. At the core of Islam is this basic confession: "There is no God but God, and Muhammad is his prophet." From the prophet, and from the book of his recitals of what God gave him to speak (the Qur'an), has arisen a world religion second only to Christianity in the number of its adherents. Both the Qur'anic form of Islam and the subsequent "little tradition" that Islam nurtured, especially in Sufism, have numerous archaic ingredients.

The first volume of Marshall Hodgson's noted study of Islam provides a full, rather sociologically oriented account of the world into which Muhammad came. Religiously, that world, in the narrowest sphere that directly impinged on Arabia, was shaped by Bedouin clan values. Mecca was a center of trade and also of polytheistic cult. Muhammad's innovations were to shift Arabian social allegiance to something more universal than the hereditary clan and to rivet religion to a single, world-transcending and world-creating God ("Allah"). The Qur'an records the visions, inspirations, or revelations that prompted Muhammad to his prophetic mission. Surah 53 speaks of Muhammad's being taught "by one terrible in power, very strong." Surah 81 insists that the revealer stood clear on the horizon and was not Satan. Tradition makes Gabriel the revealer. What he mediated to Muhammad, however, was the word, the book, of God. Many of the concepts in the Qur'an show an acquaintance with Jews or Christians, but to the Muslim mind the Qur'an is God's final, sealing prophecy—religion at its most perfect.

If it is proper to count angels, evil spirits (jinn), natural portents (earthquakes), and vivid scenes of heaven and hell as evidence of archaism, religion at its most perfect is significantly archaic. Though Allah completely transcends the world—so much so that he threatens to obliterate human freedom—Muslims are engaged in a warfare against unbelief that entails world-influencing spirits, both good and bad, and ultimate destiny in either Fire or the Garden. The Qur'an (Surah 17) speaks of God carrying Muhammad by night from the Mosque (of Mecca) to the farther mosque (of Jerusalem)—a rather shamanic magical flight. Several Surahs (2, 27) associate angels with magic and speak of using magic to control jinn. Later tradition developed all these Qur'anic hints, producing a full imagery of spirits, judgment, hellfire, paradise, and the prophet in heavenly flight.

Though mainstream Islam after Muhammad soon set its religious intelligence toward law (*Sharia*), orthodox theology never removed the mythic imagery that dealt in angels and jinn. Still it was devotional Islam, for which Sufism can stand, that most fully developed these and other archaic notions. Sufism had several component strands. In part it was a movement of reform that urged greater simplicity and austerity in the face of Islam's early military successes and worldly prosperity. In part it was a movement of high mysticism through which some Muslims came to intense union with the pure God. Finally, Sufism was also in part an encouragement to venerate saints, fear demon possession, and seek cures or favors from spiritual powers. By studying this latter portion of Sufism we discover Islam's most influential archaism.

An interesting beginning is with I. M. Lewis's remarks on *sar* possession among the Muslim women of Somalia. "As elsewhere in Islam, Somalis believe that anthropomorphic jinns lurk in every dark and empty corner, poised ready to strike capriciously and without warning at the unsuspecting passerby. These malevolent sprites are thought to be consumed by envy and greed, and to hunger especially after dainty foods, luxurious clothing, jewellery, perfume, and other finery" (p. 75). The affliction of Somali women by *sars* (jinn) somewhat redresses the social injustices they suffer, for men completely dominate Somali society; women have little official power. Men control most of the wealth; women have little security, for men may divorce women as they wish. Nevertheless, a woman possessed by a *sar* is not responsible for her actions. When the going gets rough, many women, especially wives of wealthy husbands, fall prey to *sars* who force them to spend money on clothes, parties, and the like.

Lewis gives a typical case of Somali *sar* possession. The wife of a well-to-do official with fifty pounds of ready cash in the house was depressed. A woman *sar* specialist (shamaness) convinced the wife that her depression was a possession that would only lift if she used the fifty pounds for a cathartic dance ceremony. Quickly they bought the food, summoned the participants, and began the dance/party. When the husband came home at noon, he found a hubbub. The women locked him out (for his presence could anger the *sar*), and he went off muttering. Still, he permitted the party, as though tacitly acknowledging that it repaired his wife's inferior situation a little. Similar possessions, based on a similar sociology, occur in the Muslim Sudan, Egypt, parts of North Africa, and Arabia, including Mecca. (See Lewis, p. 79.)

Another Muslim phenomenon that shows archaic roots is the veneration of saints. Ignaz Goldziher relates this phenomenon to non-Arab beliefs. In his own words: "In no other field has the original doctrine of Islam subordinated itself in such a degree to the needs of its confessors, who were Arabs only in a small minority, as in the field which is the subject of the present study: the veneration of saints" (p. 27). Though orthodoxy placed a chasm between Allah and anything created, and denied vehemently that Muhammad was the son of God, later Muslim faith became replete with numinous saints, who often dominated popular devotion. Indeed, Muhammad became the foremost of these saints, acquiring a full range of miraculous powers. Shortly after his death the Prophet's biography began to fill with miracles of feeding the hungry, slaking the thirsty, and curing the sick. By the third century after Muhammad's death, the Andalusian theologian Ibn Hibban could say that Muhammad, though perfectly human and passible, was not subject to hunger.

Before long other Muslim worthies fed a cult that existed alongside the official worship of Allah. Ordinary people would swear by saints' names, or pray to saints when the Nile was late in rising. A saint was *wali:* the intimate, almost the blood-relative, of God. One of the characteristic marks of *wali*-ship was rapture: being swept away in devotion to God. The *wali* frequently had power over nature and so could work miracles. When he or she died, this power remained near the tomb. Further, a *wali* did not need to be modest. Irahim al-Dasugi, a preeminent saint of Muslim Egypt, said of himself: "Muhammad has given me power over the whole world, over demons, over bodies and devils, and over China and the whole East to the borders of God's lands my rule is justified" (Goldziher, p. 265).

The Sufis' support for saints was a prime reason that they came into conflict with orthodox lawyers, who regarded the cult of saints as idolatry. However, the Sufis were supported by the credulous general population. So the prodigies of saints abounded. The chief saint of Damascus, Raslan, changed the four seasons in a few hours. Other men of God changed gold to blood, existed in several places simultaneously, and gave animals, or even stones, the faculty of speech. Ibrahim b. Abham was asked by a pomegranate tree to do it the honor of eating its fruit. Other *awliya* (plural of *wali*) rode on lions, changed shape at will, were able to fly, and cured many illnesses. Women could become *awliya*, and they too manifested paranormal powers. Thus when the Nile failed to rise, the holy woman Nafisa gave the citizens of Cairo her veil to throw into the river. No sooner had it hit the water than the Nile began to rise. (Goldziher, pp. 266-84.)

93

As we mentioned, the power of Muslim saints attached to their graves. As a result, pilgrimages to the graves of saints became an important Muslim devotion. Fatima Mernissi has described how modern Muslim women have made the sanctuaries of saints a source of mutual support. When women go to a tomb to pray for a child or a cure or some blessing, they often find other women there, equally sorely pressed. Frequently these other women draw out their stories and hear their complaints. Thus an informal therapy or support group develops. Emotional support is not the sort of power that Muslim devotees of saints themselves would underscore, but it reveals some of the psychodynamics at work among women who flock to the sanctuaries.

Among Berber Muslims of Morocco, whose devotion to saints is especially intense, the power underscored is *baraka*. In virtue of *baraka* one becomes a *marabout,* a holy man or saint. A story about Lyusi, a famous Moroccan *marabout,*, illustrates *baraka* and also how Sufi piety often overturns ordinary secular instincts. When Lyusi met his teacher ben Nasir, the teacher was critically ill with a loathsome smallpox. The old teacher's disciples were so repelled by his disease that none of them would wash his nightshirt. But Lyusi took the garment to a spring, washed it out, and then drank the foul water it produced. When he brought the nightshirt back to the teacher, his eyes were aflame as though he had drunk a powerful wine. Lyusi's deed exemplifies the physical courage, personal loyalty, and "ecstatic moral intensity" that *baraka* and holiness imply in Morocco (Geertz, pp. 32-33).

Anthropologist Clifford Geertz has juxtaposed Moroccan and Indonesian Islam to show the diversities a single name must cover. Because of its heavy influence rom India, the tone of Indonesian Islam is rather quietistic. Nonetheless, it too has an appetite for holy men, and, as in Morocco, they are often wonder-workers. Sunan Bonang is a noted Indonesian holy man. When accosted by a thief with a dagger, he laughed and pointed to a tree. "Do not be attached to money," he said.

"Look! There is a tree of money." The thief looked behind him and saw a tree turned to gold and hung with jewels. Marveling, he hungered for spiritual power like Bonang's and so the holy man told him to wait by the side of the river until he returned. The thief waited (forty years, by some accounts), lost in thought. When Bonang returned, he asked the thief many questions. As a result of his long meditation, the thief answered them all perfectly. Bonang therefore sent him to spread the doctrine of Islam, though the former thief had never seen the Qur'an, entered a mosque, or heard a prayer. By his reform and spiritual power he had become a Muslim. Indonesian Islam *is* reform and spiritual power.

As Annemarie Schimmel's recent study shows, the mystical dimension of Islam has been more than wonder-working. Genuine sheiks, such as the one studied by Martin Lings, could draw on a profound spirituality. But the mystical orders that developed dervish dances and other ecstatic methods took a step back toward archaic enthusiasm. Often the common people needed only that step to look on the sheiks as miracle-makers and place them amid their saints, jinn, and angels. Miracle making, like cosmological myth making, is congenial to the archaic mind. The more consubstantial the ranks of creation, the more powerful the intermediate plane of spirits and demons. Then it is not hard to get in touch with the dead or seek paranormal powers. Then there are in fact many gods beside God, and Muhammad's prophecy has been diluted.

Summary: Archaism in the World Religions

For Buddhism, Christianity, and Islam, the archaic religious mind remained most potent in the "little tradition." Among peasant peoples, or peoples poorly educated, native beliefs, existing before the world religions, usually lived on. Sometimes they had to go underground. At other times they fused with the world religion. Only rarely were they eradicated.

The cult of saints illustrates some of the similarities, differences, and complexities in the archaism of Buddhism, Christianity, and Islam. For Buddhism, the *bodhisattva* was seldom a historical figure. Thus Kuan-yin, the motherly protectress of East Asia, had no real biography. She was rather a version of the Madonna or Mother Goddess that the human psyche regularly projects. In Japan many *bodhisattvas* were indistinguishable from *kami*, the native Shinto spirit-forces. In China *bodhisattvas,* Confucian saints, and Taoist holy men fused similarly. Buddhist saints, then, functioned as personifications of divine power—as forces closer to the common person than nirvana or buddhahood. Insofar as nirvana represents a transcendence of archaic thought, a leap beyond the cosmological myth, the core of Buddhism is postarchaic. Insofar as the Buddhist masses depended on Kuan-yin, Tara, Avalokitesvara, or other saints for their real religious sustenance, the body of Buddhism has been somewhat archaic.

Christian saints supposedly were wholly different from the Christian God. Indeed, theologians distinguished between *latria*, the worship due only to God, and *dulia*, the reverence saints might receive. But in practice many Christians treated the Virgin Mary, or saints such as Francis and Jude, as their major religious resource. When such treatment glorified the saint's miraculous powers, feeding on imaginative lore, it was close to an archaic reverence for a powerful shaman, or even for powers of nature. The saint, whom the Christian devotee did not know personally, represented powers of healing, good luck, or fertility. Very easily, then, could relics of the saints become amulets or talismans. I was in Italy in the summer of 1976, when the blood of Saint Januarius, kept in Naples, failed to liquify on schedule. The people were incensed, hurling curses and threats at the saint. The attending cardinal said the miracle probably failed to occur because so many people were voting Communist. It was a bizarre scene, far from

Christianity's central doctrines or twofold command. Nevertheless, it probably represented the Christian "little tradition" quite accurately.

Since Muslim saints have less official sanction than Christian Saints, their influence is even stronger testimony to the "little tradition's" power. Indeed, the lore of Muslim saints may surpass the lore of Buddhist *bodhisattvas* and Christian saints. The starkest monotheism, then, was no match for the human need for prodigies. It was not enough for Allah to be compassionate and merciful, as it was not enough for Jesus to rise or for Buddha to disclose enlightenment-being. Rather, Muhammad's secondary concern with angels and jinn was enough for the little tradition to make them central, as were Jesus's secondary concern with demons and Buddha's with Mara. For the spirit of the ordinary Buddhist, Christian, and Muslim hungered after vivid experience. This hunger is one definition of the archaic mind: equating the vividly experienced—seen, dreamed, imagined—with the real. In each of these world religions the founder implied that the real chastens the vividly experienced and finally exceeds it. In each of these world religions the high tradition denied that man is the measure. Yet for the little tradition the measure remained human need. The world religions are therefore many great blendings of the high tradition with the little tradition.

Bibliography

Bowker, John. *The Religious Imagination and the Sense of God.* Oxford, England: Clarendon Press, 1978.

Conze, Edward. *Buddhist Scriptures.* Baltimore: Penguin, 1959.

Daly, Mary. *Gyn/Ecology.* Boston: Beacon, 1978

Deren, Maya. *Divine Horsemen: The Living Gods of Haiti.* New York: Book Collectors Society, 1952.

Earhart, H. Byron. *Religion in the Japanese Experience: Sources and Interpretations.* Belmont, Calif.: Dickenson, 1974.

Eliade, Mircea. *Shamanism.* Princeton: Princeton University Press, 1964.

———.*Zalmoxis: The Vanishing God.* Chicago: University of Chicago Press, 1972.

————.*Occultism, Witchcraft, and Cultural Fashions*. Chicago: University of Chicago Press, 1976.

Geertz, Clifford. *Islam Observed*. Chicago: University of Chicago Press, 1968.

Goldziher, Ignaz. *Muslim Studies, Volume II*. New York: Atherton, 1971.

Hodgson, Marshall G.S. *The Venture of Islam, Volume I*. Chicago, University of Chicago Press, 1974.

Jeremias, Joachim. *New Testament Theology: The Proclamation of Jesus*. New York: Charles Schribner's Sons, 1971.

Kelsey, Morton. *Discernment: A Study in Ecstasy and Evil*. New York: Paulist, 1978.

Lewis, I. M. *Ecstatic Religion*. Baltimore: Penguin, 1971.

Lings, Martin. *A Sufi Saint of the Twentieth Century*. 2d ed. Berkeley: University of California Press, 1971.

Mernissi, Fatima. "Women, Saints, and Sanctuaries." *Signs* (Autumn 1977), 101-12.

Oakes, Maud. *The Two Crosses of Todos Santos*. Princeton: Bollingen/Princeton, 1969.

Robinson, Richard, and Johnson, Willard. *The Buddhist Religion*. 2d ed. Belmont: Dickenson, 1977.

Schillebeeckx, Edward. *Jesus: An Experiment in Christology*. New York: Seabury, 1979.

Schimmel, Annemarie. *Mystical Dimensions of Islam*. Chapel Hill, N.C.: University of North Carolina Press, 1975.

Smith, Huston. *Forgotten Truth: The Primordial Tradition*. New York: Harper & Row, 1976.

Spiro, Melford E. *Buddhism and Society: A Great Tradition and Its Burmese Vicissitudes*. New York: Harper & Row, 1970.

Vermes, Geza. *Jesus the Jew*. London: Collins, 1973.

Voegelin, Eric. *Order and History: Volume IV*. Baton Rouge: Louisiana State University Press, 1974.

Waley, Arthur, trans. *Monkey*. New York: Grove Press, 1958.

Warren, Henry Clarke. *Buddhism in Translations*. New York: Atheneum, 1973.

Yang, C. K. *Religion in Chinese Society*. Berkeley: University of California Press, 1970.

PART II
Archaic Religion Today

Part II deals with archaic peoples of the recent past, whose traditions still impinge on their lives today. Sometimes these traditions are lamented. Sometimes they reflect a paradise lost. But always they offer a glimpse of a rich world-view only lately come into crisis. Always they suggest another way that people have grown to be very human.

Chapter 4:
American Indian Religion

Diversity and Unity

"It is estimated that there were up to two thousand separate cultures in the Northern Hemisphere before the advent of the white man. Many of these groups spoke mutually unintelligible languages. Anthropologists estimate that there were as many as eighty such languages in the Pacific Northwest alone" (Toelken, p. 9). From the start, then, we must realize that "American Indian religion" is another of those abstractions we use to organize complicated experience or data. The tribes of North America, which are our main focus here, ran a full gamut of social complexity, while Indians of Central and South America (Incan, Mayan, Aztec) produced systems so full that they qualify in many taxonomies as high cultures. Of the North American diversity Hultkrantz says: "The simple hunting religion of the Naskapi Indians of Labrador contrasts sharply with the intricate horticultural religion of Pueblo Indians of New Mexico and Arizona, and the simple structure of the Californian Indian religions bears little resemblance to the religion of sacred kingship represented by the Natchez on the lower Mississippi" (p 3).

Thus it is the unity of American Indian religion that presents scholars their problem; the diversity is manifest. Faithful to the divergent details of the different tribes' beliefs and ceremonies, and weak on theory that could root religion in universally human drives, the anthropologists who have done most of the research have been hard pressed to focus the whole. We shall spend considerable time on American Indian rituals and endeavor to illustrate the rich import of American Indian ecology (interaction with the natural environment). Before and after these major concerns, however, we shall focus on sources of unity. The case study of contemporary American Indian children that comes after our studies of ritual and ecology suggests that many American Indians early began what can only be called an erotic relation with nature. Their souls went out, both admiringly and with desire, to the beauty and goodness of the physical world. That world was eminently alive, eminently real, and the ultimate warrant for judging human existence good. It so beguiled American Indians, in all the times and places for which we have data, that it provides a base line—a strongly unifying point of reference.

Before launching our study of American Indian rituals and ecology, however, let us contemplate several other sources of unity—several other perspectives that can help us keep the whole in view. First, there is the correlation between religion and meaning that we made previously. Both culturally and personally, American Indians, like premodern peoples everywhere, dealt with the deepest issues of their lives religiously. The powers that merited most serious attention and the human experiences that demanded most reflection evoked a holistic and reverent response. The powers of life and death, summer and winter, sun and rain, health and sickness, begot myths, ceremonies, and tacit convictions that we can only call religious. For American Indians these powers were mysterious: too full to understand with the upper mind, intelligible only by communion from the heart. Experiences of birth and death, love and hate, work and war, reinforced this religious attitude. The ultimate meaning of these and like human experiences slid into the rhythms and mysteries of nature. They were times when the deepest power, perhaps even the divinity of the world, confronted human beings and demanded adaptation. Were birth or death to occur unharmonized with nature's rhythms and divinity, it would be worse than painful, for worse than pain is a life out of sorts with *orenda* or *wakan,* the holy force that charges the world. Such a life is meaningless: threatening, flat, profane. It is not a life in which human beings can sing and dance; it is no life at all.

Second, one can observe that all American Indian tribes possessed a variety of religious conceptions. Most tribes had no word for religion itself, but all tribes had deities, ceremonies, and convictions about either the supernatural or the holy.

Third, Hultzkrantz and others have used some qualities of American Indian religious culture to distinguish this culture from what they sometimes call Old World (usually European, Indian, or Asian) religious cultures. These qualities are not universal throughout the Americas, or even throughout North America, but they recur frequently enough to be called characteristic. Most outstanding are the rigorous asceticism and individualism that American Indians have shown. They express a strength of mind that has impressed comparativists as distinctive. Old World archaic religions, on the whole, have not disciplined the average tribal member as American Indians have, nor have they given the individual status over the group. In their vision quests and warrior rituals, American Indians made the flesh pay huge debts to the spirit. In the dignity and honor they accorded individual rectitude, American Indians taught each person to be responsible for that spirit.

Perhaps the most celebrated ceremony that expresses this American Indian strength of mind is the sun dance of the Oglala Sioux (Brown, pp. 67-100). In it adults offered their bodies as a sacrifice on behalf of the tribe. With rich symbolism the people would erect a cottonwood tree in the center of a circle—the circle represented both the whole of creation and the whole of the tribe. After that they would erect other posts and to them tie rawhide thongs that were bound into the flesh of the dancers' shoulders, breasts, and backs. The dancers—both men and women—then danced until the thongs broke out from their flesh. The explanation by Black Elk that Brown records is worth quoting: "the flesh represents ignorance, and, thus, as we dance and break the thong loose, it is as if we were being freed from the bonds of the flesh. It is much the same as when you break a young colt; at first a halter is necessary, but later when he has become broken, the rope is no longer necessary. We too are young colts when we start to dance, but soon we become broken and submit to the Great Spirit" (p. 85).

Other qualities that confer some unity on American Indians' religion are their concepts of the supernatural and of a high god, their three-tiered view of the world, and their nature gods and spirits. Many tribes had a distinct word for the supernatural and distinguished between the sacred and the profane. For them the supernatural was distant from the natural; it was more likely to occur in dreams than in waking life. It also tended to disrupt the natural; thus, changes of weather (storms, wind), new constellations in the heavens, and the masked dances of cult societies were all regarded as extraordinary and unexplainable. The supernatural also might break into the natural as a powerful psychological experience—a vision, vivid dream, or scary encounter with an animal.

The supernatural was more universal among American Indians than the concept of a high god, yet this concept very likely was quite archaic. Although scholars dispute this thesis, Hultzkrantz provides considerable evidence for it. (See pp. 15-26.) For example, indications are that the Yahgan Indians of Tierra del Fuego traced their concept of the high god back eight thousand years. He was Watauniewa, "the old, eternal, unchangeable one." Watauniewa was invisible, ruled all alone, and gave the Yahgan their ethics. Though not a creator god, he ruled life and death, apportioned food to human beings, and presided over the puberty rites of both males and females. The Yahgan prayed both formally and informally to Watauniewa, offering him petitions as well as thanks. They never sacrificed to him, however, because he already owned everything that existed.

Although Watauniewa was typical of most American Indian high gods in not being the creator, some tribes did have a creator high god. For north-central California tribes the high god even created *ex nihilo* by the power of his speech. For the Uitoto of Colombia, the god Nainuema created by clutching "the appearance" to his breast, protecting it, and fashioning it into the earth. Other tribes related the high god to the "master of the animals" or the cosmic pillar (two archaic shamanic themes). Thus the Mascouten prayed to the Great Spirit before and after the hunt, giving him first-fruit sacrifices. The Flathead Indians believed that a cosmic tree ran from deep in Mother Earth up to the heavens and Amotken, "the old one," lived in its top branches; he was the kind creator. At the tree's roots was the home of Amtep, the evil god.

Many tribes pictured the world itself as three-tiered, consisting of a heaven above, the earth on which humans walked, and an underworld. (Hunters were weaker on the underworld concept than agriculturalists were.) The earth might be square or round, but most tribes placed themselves at its center. The Beaver Indians were distinctive in giving the three tiers a cruciform shape, while some Mississippi tribes thought of the world as a cross within a circle. The cross represented the four directions and the four winds; the circle was a common symbol for totality.

Finally, most tribes reverenced nature gods and spirits; the sun, the moon, and the stars were normally deities (or perhaps symbols of deities). The Natchez Indians of the lower Mississippi had a complete theocracy, headed by the priest-chief who led the sun clan. In the chief's temple burned eternal fire, symbol of the supreme being: the sun. The Crow Indians of Montana also regarded the sun as the supreme being, though Old Man Coyote later replaced him in their mythology. Many tribes considered thunder the voice of the gods, and almost all tribes populated the world with spirits, represented by birds or animals. Many tribes considered Mother Earth the source of all life. The Cagaba of northern Colombia made their feminine motif explicit. "Woman is the most elementary expression of fertility and the most exalted deity of culture; she is the Mother, the creator. From her are born mankind, the good black earth, the edible plants, the animals, and all nature. All these elements are 'Children of the Mother' and are subject to her 'law' (Hultzkrantz, p. 53). In North America the Fox Indians said that the earth on which humans lived was a woman, while the Lenape said that the earth was a goddess or contained a goddess. Thus the Shahaptin chief Smohalla spoke for many American Indians when, refusing to plow the earth, he asked, "Shall I take a knife and tear my mother's bosom?"

American Indian Rituals

Like archaic peoples everywhere, American Indians acted out their beliefs ritualistically. In general they celebrated both changes in nature and changes in the life-cycle. Planting, harvesting, the opening of the hunting season, solstices, and new seasons—all required special observances. Although normally the whole tribe participated in nature ceremonies, ceremonies for the lifecycle tended to be private. Some exceptions to this principle, such as the Apache communal puberty rite for girls and the burial of a notable brave, probably would entail the participation of the whole tribe. Usually, however, birth, puberty, marriage and funerary rites focused on the individual.

Both nature and individual rites played with cosmological themes. Life and fertility, for example, played back and forth between the human and the natural. Thus the New Year ritual that renewed the tribe's fertility might require a sacred lodge that replicated the universe. The curing ceremony for a sick woman usually begged the natural elements to lend her their healing power and the Great Spirit to put her back in harmony with the natural whole.

To keep our study to manageable portions, let us concentrate on American Indian rituals for the life-cycle. First are the attitudes and ceremonies bearing on birth. The Lakotas were representative in stressing the importance of parental kindness and love, which were based on the spouses' mutual love. "The first thing a dutiful husband did in the morning, after breakfast, was to arrange his wife's hair and to paint her face" (Hamilton, p. 18). If the husband was to be at home, he worked with the women to lighten their load. Social pressure mounted strongly against the man who unduly scolded his wife or beat her or the children; he was considered a weakling, a coward, a man unfit to have a family. (The Lakotas tended to limit the number of their children to four or five, spacing them by abstinence.) Children also had influence on their parents, a right to care and love. Horse Looking, a Lokota with a severe drinking problem, was a terror when in his cups. Taming him was easy, however, because one only needed to place his youngest child in his arms. Immediately he would calm down and forget his rage, petting and fondling the child (Hamilton, p. 19).

Among the Sioux a pregnant woman tended to spend considerable time alone so that she could wander in beautiful natural scenes and let them influence the fetus. She avoided certain animals, lest the child receive their features; a rabbit, for instance, might give the child a harelip. The mother also mused regularly on the exploits of a great figure she had chosen as a model for her child, and when the child was born many of the first lullabies it heard stressed the hero's virtues.

The Ojibwa of western Ontario held a naming feast shortly after a child's birth. Among the guests would be several persons renowned for their spiritual powers of naming. Each of them would give the child a cryptic name related to his own vision quest, and also a symbolic gift. A tiny cane might signify long life, a tiny gun a great hunter. These gifts would be hung above the cradle, while the names would be a protection throughout life. Naming among Eskimo tribes tended to be for the ancestor whose soul had been reincarnated in the child. Eskimo parents rarely abused their children, for that would insult the ancestor, perhaps causing it to depart and kill the child.

Navaho Indians focused on the birth itself, seeing it as a time for joy and thanksgiving. The mother sat on a sheepskin in the hogan, linked by a belt to a post or beam. Her mother, sister, and female relatives would attend her, holding her hips and knees. Sometimes a shaman would be present, but only for spiritual aid. After birth an attendant would tie the cord and bind the child with a fungus. Then she would take it outside and wash it with suds of the yucca plant in a pile of ashes. The mother then would drink a thin gruel prepared by her sister or sister-in-law. All those who performed such services would be paid—in sheep, buckskin, hides, blankets, horses, or the like. The greater the payment, the sooner the woman would recover. Those in attendance would rub the child with sage and sing over it to bless it. At the naming ceremony, when the child was two or three months old, the grandparents usually gave the name.

Different tribes dealt with the fearsome aspects of birth differently. Some Central American tribes sent women who died in childbirth to a special heaven, where they lived with the sun god and cared for bold warriors. Frequently the pregnant woman had to avoid meat lest the souls of the game be offended and avoid the huntsman. In other tribes she could not scratch lest the fetus have diseased skin, nor look at passersby directly lest her power afflict them. Although the importance of birth made it a time when supernatural forces drew near, American Indians seldom considered it defiling, as some other peoples did (for instance, archaic Chinese). Though the mother-to-be usually was under some restrictions, the father-to-be sometimes shared them. (Underhill,

1965, pp. 59-60.) In general, then, birth was a happy time.

Puberty rites were a way of making a boy or girl ready for marriage, frequently by a "rebirth" into adulthood. They also might be the occasion for initiation into tribal lore. Among the Navaho, *kinalda*, the first menses, called for a four-day ceremony, only the last night of which was public. The mythic rationale for the ceremony focused on Changing Woman, the most important Navaho divinity. During the four days, the girl did not wash her hair, and she constantly ground corn (to make her industrious). She could have no meat, sweets, or favorite foods, only unsalted corn-based foods. No water could touch her lips; she had to drink through a tube. She could neither scratch herself nor sleep very much; when she did sleep, it was only on her back. At the concluding ceremony she was bathed, dressed, and made to lie face down on a blanket, where she was kneaded into (adult) shape by an adult female. Her hair was dressed ceremonially, and she was given babies to handle, for her touch could make them grow faster. A corncake was baked for those who kept vigil with the girl, and many songs were sung. Toward the end of the last evening, near daybreak, the medicine man would paint her face red and daub white clay on her cheeks. The girl then would race twelve young men about a half mile, and if she won she could expect great good luck.

Most other female puberty rites blended disciplinary features, designed to impress the young woman with the duties that adulthood imposes, and fertility features, to underscore the power of motherhood. For all tribes the "woman-power" that came with menstruation was potent. Many tribes had menstrual taboos and sequestered women from men during their periods. Yet these taboos seldom implied that blood was defiling. Rather, it was powerful, the source of life, and so not to be crossed with male hunting power, the source of death. Alternatively, their blood gave women a natural sacrality, often on the model of the fertility-sacrality of Mother Earth.

Marriage was less prominent ceremonially than puberty. Speaking of North American marriage overall, Driver says: "North American Indians exhibit an amazing variety of ways to acquire a mate, of forms of marriage such as polygamy, of incest taboos, of postnuptial residence customs, of parent-in-law relations, and of family structure" (p. 222). As among most nonliterate peoples, the Indians regarded marriage as a contract between two groups of kin rather than between two individuals. Different tribes weighted these factors differently, however. The tribes of the Arctic, Sub-Arctic, Great Basin, and Northeast Mexico—areas more primitive economically—tended to give the individuals more weight. Areas more advanced economically gave greater weight to the opinion of elders (Driver, p. 222).

Many tribes betrothed infants or young children, sometimes making partial payment of the bride-price at that time. Usually virginity was desirable, though more often than not tribes tolerated premarital sexual relations. The Cheyenne and Crow especially insisted on virginity (for the bride), while northwest costal tribes sometimes confined young women from first menstruation to marriage, since virginity (like a light complexion) would bring a higher bride-price or enable the girl to marry into a higher ranking family. The early age at which marriage usually took place (early teens for girls, a few years older for boys) lessened problems of premarital chastity, as did the fact that births outside wedlock carried little stigma.

A man could acquire a wife by paying a bride-price or by working for the woman's father. The concept of bride-price was strongest on the plains, prairies, and northwest coast, where sometimes it became a matter of pride or prestige to pay generously. Some tribes in Mexico and Central America enacted a mock capture of women as part of the marital ceremony. A southeastern couple who wanted to marry but found their desire thwarted by elders might elope. Were they able to avoid recapture until the harvest festival, they could then appear together and be accepted as man and wife. "All offenses short of murder were annually forgiven by this culture at this time, and elopement was less serious than many other wrongs" (Driver, p. 226).

Slightly more than half the North American tribes favored an extended family, and among the western Pueblos, Midatsa-Mandans, and Iroquois, matrilocal extended families were the rule. In these groups women owned the houses and farmland, and descent was traced through them. The husband had little say about his children, and a woman could divorce him by dropping his hat outside the door.

Though women and men obviously were coordinated to one another, their marriage itself rarely revealed new religious truths. Thus few tribes made marriage a symbol for divinity or for their relationship with divinity. Revelations of identity came rather in each sex's puberty rites. As female puberty rites focused on woman-power, so male puberty rites focused on male-powers. Among the Papago, men needed purifying at three times: after war, after eagle killing, and after a salt pilgrimage (Underhill, 1969, pp. 165-252). These were times when the power men had gained at puberty came into crisis, and so the purifying rites on these occasions were renewals of the puberty rite.

Warrior who slew enemies (fighting in self-defense) came into dangerous contact with the supernatural. They had to stop fighting (the killing had exhausted their strength), blacken their faces, and stay apart from the rest of the tribe as persons tabooed. Upon return home these warriors had to stay in seclusion for sixteen days, attended by a guardian who gave them instruction in the significance of what they had done. Their wives shared this seclusion, not by staying with the warriors, but by assuming menstrual taboos. At the end of the seclusion period the warrior and his wife would fast and spend the last night sitting upright without moving. Then they would join a victory dance at which the warrior would brandish the scalp he had taken, thus establishing it as a powerful fetish.

The salt pilgrimage was a journey to salt deposits at beaches on the northern Gulf of California. It was an arduous trip, requiring fasting and minimal consumption of water. The Papago turned this traditional journey into a ritual, making its hardships a way of obtaining power.

Warriors had to be purified after killing eagles because they gained power through such killing. In seclusion they would learn eagle songs from a guardian, and the eagle's spirit would come to them in dreams.

Power, then, dominated most male rituals, especially the power to kill. To acquire this power for warfare or hunting, males fasted, endured austerities, and sought intimacy with tutelary spirits. Frequently male puberty rites blended with initiation into male groups (sodalities), during which boys were schooled in tribal cosmology, religious lore, or curing techniques. The age of the initiates ranged from ten years and up, and the initiations tended to occur annually or every seven years. The Aztec sodalities were the most elaborate. At fifteen years of age all Aztec boys left home and went to live in a boarding school. There they received instruction in farming, arts and crafts, bearing arms, Aztec history and religion, and the duties of citizenship. They formed work parties to cultivate public lands and build public works, and they served in the army, making up the bulk of the Aztec fighting force (Driver, p. 358).

Other male initiations entailed fighting, starving, taking drugs, and torture. Sioux rites stressed fasting and being sent on frightening missions—the preparation of hardy warriors. So initiation for boys stressed discipline more than sexual matters. Male coming of age was less dramatic than female, and male fertility less obvious. The power men needed from the spirits was fearlessness, endurance, and self-control, for men dealt with death intimately. They also needed religious lore about plants, animals, and tribal customs, for all the adult Indian's interactions with nature, and most of his tribe's customs, were religious.

South American burial rites placed the corpse in the ground (Amazon area) or used coffins for burial above ground. North American tribes east of the Rocky Mountains exposed the corpse on a platform. Trees, coffins, and cairns (heaps of stones) were other burial places. Some tribes on the West Coast practiced cremation. In the Amazon secondary burial was often used: when the flesh had decomposed the Indians dug up the bones and placed them in an urn. The Iroquois and Algonguin in North America practiced secondary burial, with the added feature that every ten or twelve years they dug up the remains of all who had died in that period and placed them in a communal grave (Hultkrantz, pp. 137-39).

Belief in reincarnation was widespread among American Indians and a major tenet among Eskimos. Still, burial customs suggest that though Indians both loved and feared the dead, they did not worship them. Exceptions to this rule occurred in South American tribes close to Andean high culture. In North America the Hopi had a cult of *kachinas* and the Zuni a cult of *koko*—rain and fertility spirits who woke deceased ancestors. Finally, the medicine men of some tribes used the dead as guardian spirits, but this practice was not the rule.

Since death was a fearsome event, American Indians considered undesirable a house in which death occurred. The house was abandoned, destroyed, or moved for fear of the ghost of the deceased. In North America death usually required the sacrifice of a horse or dog belonging to the deceased. During some periods of Central and South American history, the death of an important person required the sacrifice of a human being—a slave, war captive, child of a civic-minded person, or the deceased's widow.

The Navaho would take a dying person to an unused hogan, dress him in his best clothes, and keep watch with only a small band. (They considered this watch dangerous.) After death the attendants would wash the corpse and leave it in the shade. While some cleaned the hogan, removing all footprints to confuse the ghost, other attendants dug a grave or prepared a crevice in a canyon. (See Reichard, pp. 141-43.) Mourners had to be silent. They could not spit or turn a stone. On the trip home they skipped, hopped, and took a circular route, to hasten the spirit's trip to the other world.

Many tribes consigned their dead to another world, and frequently their shamans guided the dead on this journey (served as "psychopomps"). The theory was that each person had two souls: one that gave life to the body, and another that was free to travel. It might travel in dreams, shamanic ecstasy, or after death. Because the soul might also leave the body in sickness, the shamanic healer's task often was to counter soul-loss. When the other principal cause of sickness was the presence of a foreign object, the healer's function was to determine (frequently by trance) where this object was and remove it.

Eliade has described the healing techniques of shamans among the Paviotso of western North America (1964, pp. 302-5). The shaman first asked about the patient's actions before the illness. Then he directed that a stick be placed upright beside the patient's head. It had to be three or four feet long, made of willow wood, and decorated at the top with an eagle feather, which the shaman supplied (the feather probably represented the shaman's magical flight—his ability to leave the body and go to the land of the spirits). The shaman did his crucial work while in trance. If he had to go on a journey to pursue a lost soul, he narrated his experiences to the assembled community. Usually these experiences provided symbols relevant to diagnosis and cure. For instance, if the shaman saw fresh flowers, a cure was certain. If the flowers were faded, death would occur. When a foreign object had caused the illness, the trance revealed it. Then, having recovered consciousness, the shaman, removed the foreign object, usually by sucking it out. The typical ceremony included many songs and often ended with a dance. Before leaving the shaman gave the family instructions for the patient's continued care—what diet he should receive, what designs they should paint on his body, and so forth.

American Indian Ecology

The seasonal, life-cycle, and healing rites of American Indians all implied a close relationship with nature. The shaman's consciousness displayed this ecology dramatically, for he who supplied an eagle feather, as part of the paraphernalia of curing, most likely "became" that eagle when he took magical flight. Similarly, the vision quest that many tribes practiced at puberty brought the young person into contact with spirits who took animal form. The vision was prepared by fasting and solitude, and it gave the recipient a lifelong orientation. Two Leggings' story of Bear White Child shows a young boy obtaining his vision:

> One day, as the boy was resting on a rock, a bird appeared and told him to be ready because Bear Up Above was going to adopt him. The bird said he should not be afraid; Bear Up Above would not hurt him. As the boy remained on the rock, watching the setting sun, he noticed a black cloud, as if a storm were about to break. The cloud grew larger and more threatening. He felt strong gusts of wind and saw streaks of lightning. It began to rain very hard and he was afraid the large hailstones would kill him. As he ran for a place to hide, a voice told him not to fear, that he was about to be adopted. The hail fell all around, but the boy was not touched. Again he looked in the direction the storm had come; a black cloud hung in the middle of the hail. The cloud's center began taking shape and he saw the head of Bear Up Above. At the moment the upper half of the bear's body appeared, the hail stopped. The bear sang a song as it reached down to embrace the boy. It lifted him up into the air and when it finished singing, put him down. (Momaday, p. 23)

From visions such as these, American Indians got tokens— bear sinews, eagle feathers, rabbits' feet, and the life—that became ingredients of their medicine bundles, their repositories of power-objects that could cure.

Living within the cosmological myth, having a sense that animals, plants, and humans were kin, American Indians felt bonded to the seasons, the elements, and all living things. The Naskapi of Labrador reflected this feeling in their view of hunting. At the world's beginning, animals lived in tribes and could talk. Even when human beings came upon earth and began hunting animals in order to survive, animals remained the spiritual equals of human beings. As one Naskapi song put it, "You and I wear the same covering and have the same mind and spiritual strength" (Eliade, 1967, p. 173). Animals that the hunters killed would be reincarnated, for they had immortal souls. The hunter dealt with sacred things and therefore had to treat the bones of slain animals reverently. To disregard hunting taboos willfully was to sin seriously.

A Thompson myth spoke of the sun as father of the Indians and of the earth as their mother. At death human beings returned to Mother Earth, being covered with her flesh in a blanket under which their bones could rest in peace. This human fate ultimately was due to Old One, who had changed Earth Woman into the present-day earth. Earth Woman's hair became the trees and grasses, her flesh became the clay. Her bones turned into rocks, her blood became springs of water. The Old One told Earth Woman: "You will be as the mother of people, for from you their bodies will spring, and to you they will go back. People will live as in your bosom, and sleep in your lap. They will derive nourishment from you, and they will utilize all parts of your body" (Eliade, 1967, p. 136).

The same bond between human beings and nature shows in the Dakota story of the gift of the sacred pipe. Wakantanka, the Dakota deity, sent a Maiden with the pipe. She explained its origin and purpose: it came from the deity and was to be used to bind all Indians in peace—peace with one another and peace with Wakantanka. In this context the Maiden said: "You realize that all your necessities of life come from the earth below, the sky above, and the four winds. Whenever you do anything wrong against these elements, they will always take some revenge upon you. You should reverence them" (Eliade, 1967, p. 223). In smoking the pipe, purifying themselves in the sweat-lodge, seeking a vision, dancing the sun dance, or playing their sacred ball game, the Oglala Sioux remembered this injunction and reverenced all the natural elements and directions. (See Brown.)

Hartley Burr Alexander has provided glimpses that a similar ecology obtained among agricultural peoples. Using an unknown missionary author of the seventeenth century who was commenting on Central American Indians, Alexander stresses the importance of maize: "If one look closely at these Indians he will find that everything they do and say has something to do with maize. A little more, and they would make a god of it. There is so much conjuring and fussing with their corn fields, that for them they will forget wives and children and any other pleasure, as if the only end and aim of life was to secure a crop of corn" (p. 73). In fact, many Indians did reverence maize divinities, whose sex usually was female. Thus the prehistoric change from hunting to farming that we studied earlier brought the same religious changes for archaic Americans. As Alexander puts it, "The earth-embosomed life of agricultural man is a sedentary life, and when the man-animal changes his ways from wandering after prey and from war and mastery into what we usefully term a 'productive life,' there is a certain feminization or woman-centering of his thought, and the goddesses come into their own" (Alexander, p. 81).

The preoccupation with maize that made corn maidens central for many tribes had analogies in the central foci of other tribes. Tribes who lived on the buffalo, deriving from it not only meat but clothing and housing, worshiped this animal as a powerful spirit, a god of life. Eskimos who were similarly dependent on the seal reverenced the spirit of each seal they slew. They sent their shamans to Sedna, mistress of the sea animals, promising to renew the taboos that honored the seal, to remove the community strife that made them unfit to hunt purely, and so forth.

116

So intimately did economically significant animals enter the consciousnesses of archaic peoples, and so religious were those consciousnesses, that the Plains Assiniboine put the creation of horses into their creation account, even though they did not have horses in any number until the eighteenth century. Despite this "history," the wolf-god Inktonmi made horses "in the beginning," when he made the rest of the Assiniboine world. The creation account also provides another evidence of the American Indians' concern with the animals of their habitat.

> All the earth was flooded with water. Inktonmi sent animals to dive for dirt at the bottom of the sea. No animal was able to get any. At last he sent the Muskrat. It came up dead, but with dirt in its claws. Inktonmi saw the dirt, took it, and made the earth out of it. Inktonmi was wearing a wolf-skin robe. He said, "There shall be as many months as there are hairs on this skin before it shall be summer." Frog said, "If the winter lasts as long as that, no creature will be able to live. Seven months of winter will be enough." He kept on repeating this, until Inktonmi got angry, and killed him. Still Frog stuck out seven of his toes. Finally Inktonmi consented, and said there should be seven winter months. Inktonmi then created men and horses out of dirt. Some of the Assiniboine and other northern tribes had no horses. Inktonmi told the Assiniboine that they were always to steal horses from other tribes. (Sproul, p. 253)

"Thank God for Frog," many Assiniboine must have said, and "Let's hope the other tribes know about our charter to steal their horses!"

The Cupeno of California had a distinctive creation account that featured a bag hung in space. In the beginning everything was dark and void; just the bag hung in space. When the bag opened, coyote came out from one half and wildcat from the other. They began to argue who was older. Coyote was older because he spoke first. By then people had been created, but they could not see, because they were in mud and darkness. They were not in the bag with coyote and wildcat. They arose

117

from the mud and started to sing. People heard coyote speak first, so they knew he was older. Shamans today understand coyote, because people heard him first (Sproul, p. 242).

The Mandan, who once lived in central North Dakota, had a rich creation account that exemplifies many ecological themes. In the beginning the surface of the earth was water and all was darkness. The First Creator and Lone Man were walking on top of the water when they saw a small duck. They asked her where she got her food. She told them, "From the bed of the water." Then she dived down to the bed and brought up a ball of sand. First Creator and Lone Man said, "Let us create land out of this substance, and living creatures, and let us make the land productive that it may bear fruit for the subsistence of the creatures that we shall create." They agreed to go off in different directions, create, and then come back together and compare results.

First Creator made broad valleys, hills, coulees (creek beds), mountain streams, springs, the buffalo elk, black- and white-tailed antelope, mountain sheep, "and all other creatures useful to mankind for food and clothing." He made valleys and coulees as shelters for animals too. Lone Man created level country, with lakes, small streams, and rivers far apart. Some of the animals he made lived in the water, such as beaver, otter, and muskrat; others were cattle of many colors, moose, and other land animals. When First Creator surveyed what Lone Man had made, he found it too level; it afforded humans no protection. He liked his own creation better, because it had buttes and mountains by which humans could mark their way. Also, Lone Man's lakes had no outlet and so would stagnate. Judging the animals, First Creator said: "The things I have made are far more useful to man. Look at the buffalo . . . in winter their hair grows long and shaggy, to combat the cold; in warm weather they shed their hair in order to endure the heat more comfortably." But Lone Man pointed out that he could not undo his creation. So they agreed to let human beings use both sets of creatures (Sproul, pp. 248-49).

Lone Man became the father of the Mandans, at whose head he had many adventures. His stories are "etiological myths" that explain the origin of either features of the landscape or Mandan culture. In these myths, as in all the myths of North American Indians, the great interest is the tribe's life in the land. Of course, other peoples have been interested in their life—curious about how they came into being. Much of the Hebrew Bible, for instance, concerns the origin of Israel and its customs. Shinto mythology, as found in the earliest chronicle, the *Kojiki*, concerns the first human beings, who came into existence on the Japanese Islands.

The American Indian mentality was more like the early Japanese than the early Israelite. For both Indians and early Japanese, nature was all absorbing. Israel was interested in nature, but more interested in human affairs—in history. Having inherited the Israelite line (as it developed through Jewish and Christian cultures), we modern Americans have a different ecology than did the American Indians. Our divinity, society, and individual selves stand apart from nature. Stories of the origin of our animals, whether mythological or scientific, affect us only sightly. Since their emotional impact is shallow, we have to exercise our imaginations if we are to appreciate the affect that the American Indian creation accounts carried. Neither the American Indian divinity nor the people nor the individual self stood apart from nature. Rather, Indians lived with a cluster of animals and the contour of the land. Reverence for them was not a reflective commitment, a reasoned imperative. It was an instinct: nature was holy.

Case Study: The American Indian Child

In the study of archaic peoples the predominant focus has been mature men. Unconsciously Western scholars have projected their own interests, and so produced this predominant focus. To be sure, anthropologists have worked over the social organizations of tribes and so have dealt with women,

119

children, and the aged. But the concern of scholars with political power, hunting, farming, curing, and war has tended to make women, children, and the aged somewhat peripheral. To redress this imbalance and angle into archaic religious consciousness from fresh starting points, we conclude these chapters on archaic religion today with case studies of persons outside the mainstream. The first draws on Robert Coles's work with contemporary American Indian children.

From interviews with Hopi and Pueblo children in the American Southwest, Coles has painted a beautiful picture of the American Indian child's consciousness. Despite all the influences of white culture, many traditional Indian character-istics remain. For example, more dramatically than either white or black children, American Indian children reflect nature's cyclicism, its rhythms. Regularly these children withdraw into themselves, block out the world of human affairs, and become lost in natural phenomena. One minute the white schoolteacher will find the Indian child "present," intimate and attentive, the next minute the child will have left the classroom mentally and become lost in contemplating a puffy white cloud or a tree starting to bloom. The white teacher's bewilderment usually amuses the Indian mother, who, without great deliberation, has taught her children to note a lovely cloud formation, watch the wind moving the grass, ponder the changing shapes of the shadows.

Moreover, the fluid, mutable quality of physical nature that such attention emphasizes carries over to the Indian child's view of human nature. The little girl who falls sick to her stomach learns from her mother that the sickness makes her different, a new person. As the sky becomes different by changing from clear to stormy, so the little girl becomes different by changing from a quiet stomach to an achey one. The body changes, goes through cycles, throws up signals, just like nature. To come to grips with the inner world of the stomach—and even more the inner world of the spirit—one does well to pay attention to the outer world of natural change. "No wonder Indian children are often regarded by outsiders as strangely 'philosophical,' as almost preoccupied with 'existential' questions. Indian mothers feel awe and wonder within themselves as they look upward at the sun, the moon, the stars, or across the desert toward a given mesa; those mothers make sure that their children feel the same. They are not permitted to take *any* sights and sounds for granted" (Coles, p. 517).

From their self-defining relationship with nature, Indian children absorb other important convictions. One is that immortality is more real than linear time. The return of the seasons predominates, and the uncle who walked this land many summers ago still walks it in spirit. Similarly, the storm that amazed a family five autumns ago can return tonight in a dream and so prove its continuing existence, prove the melding of past, present, and future. An Indian girl lives within this cyclic view of time because she is close to nature and nature is a living cycle. When she falls, her mother comforts her, but she also comforts the earth, smoothing it out. When the girl sits on a rock, one of her parents may well remind her that the rock belongs to the earth, and so she must use it carefully and gratefully. In the same way, the clouds belong to the sky, which generously lets us enjoy them. The wind brushes our skins, but moves on independently. Nature shares these forces; human sharing is but a reflection of nature's constant giving.

When they bring up their children to these attitudes, Indian parents are not consciously trying to inculcate an ecological sensitivity. They are just handing on the traditional, self-evident belief of their people that a sacredness permeates the whole world. In a comparativist's categories this belief is a species of pantheism: it identifies divinity with the living whole. From early childhood to old age, Indians love the beauty and reality of their divine environment erotically. By watching their parents, children absorb a contemplative wonder and awe. "A thunderstorm, a windstorm, or simply a bright, clear day—and the Pueblo or Hopi child is happy, is ready (if it were possible) to reach out and touch with great satisfaction the sun, the dark clouds, the air rushing by so noisily. Mothers extend their arms, sing the praises of what is to be seen from the door of the house. Children watch and feel impelled to do likewise" (Coles, p. 522).

Indian language reflects this pantheistic, erotic love of nature. It is figurative, poetic, full of metaphors and similes. To a white observer it seems animistic: treating all things—even rocks and waters—as though they were alive. Land that white observers consider useless desert the Indians—even Indian children—feel protective toward. They have been taught to invest themselves in the natural world, to imagine the natural world as their greatest treasure and reality. Sensitive white observers therefore come to realize that the Indian child sees a different sky and earth than they do. How different it is the observers can never know, but it is different enough to give them pause. For example, the Hopi or Pueblo child shows little inclination to be possessive about nature; unlike white culture, Indian culture has not needed to fill the earth and subdue it. Nature has invited the Indian to harmony, not exploitation. The Indian's response has been religion, not business.

From this religious response arises what the white observer may consider aloofness or impersonalism. Trying to commune with nature, an Indian child appears uncommunicative to other human beings. Indian speech is sparse, because so much time and energy go into tacit, holistic efforts to "be with" nature or other tribal members from the heart. Thomas Whitecloud has described going back to his people's silent communication after he had been at a white boarding school:

> The dance stops. The men walk back to the walls and talk in
> low tones or with their hands. There is little conversation, yet
> everyone seems to be sharing some secret. A woman looks at a
> small boy wandering away, and he comes back to her. Strange,

I think, and then remember. These people are not sharing words—they are sharing a mood. Everyone is happy. I am so used to white people that it seems strange so many people could be together without someone talking. These Indians are happy because they are together, and because the night is beautiful outside, and the music is beautiful. I try hard to forget school and white people, and be one of these—my people. I try to forget everything but the night, and it is part of me; that I am one with my people and we are all a part of something universal. (Momaday, p 67)

The future life, the eternity beyond death, will be joining not just present tribal members but ancestors as well. One will be with them, be part of the fullness of nature. Then the seasons will never end, and the trials of present times will be no more. Then all that separates one from holy nature, that disturbs one's communion, will be removed. In terms that we developed earlier, the future to which American Indians still point their children is a fulfilling participation in the cosmological myth. The bondedness of creation, its consubstantiality, makes the Indian group enjoying the dance feel at one. It makes the mother observing the storm raise her hands in pure delight. Despite all the depradations of white Americans, American Indians continue to enjoy a beautiful archaic intimacy with their land.

Bibliography

Alexander, Hartley Burr. *The World's Rim*. Lincoln, Nebraska: University of Nebraska Press, 1953.

Ballinger, Franchot. "The Responsible Center: Man and Nature in Pueblo and Navaho Ritual Songs and Prayers." *American Quarterly*, XXX/1 (Spring 1978). 90-107.

Boas, Franz. *The Central Eskimo*. Lincoln, Nebraska: University of Nebraska Press, 1964.

Brown, Joseph Epes, ed. *The Sacred Pipe*. Baltimore: Penguin, 1971.

Coles, Robert. *Eskimos, Chicanos, Indians: Volume IV of Children of Crisis*. Boston: Little, Brown & Company, 1977.

Driver, Harold E. *Indians of North America*. Chicago: University of Chicago Press, 1961.

Eliade, Mircea. *Shamanism*. Princeton: Princeton University Press, 1964.
————. *From Primitives to Zen*. New York: Harper & Row, 1967.
Fox, J. R. "Religions of Illiterate Peoples: North America." in *Historia Religionum*, II, edited by C. Jouco Bleeker and G. Widengren. Leiden: E. J. Brill, 1971, pp. 593-608.
Hamilton, Charles, ed. *Cry of the Thunderbird*. Norman, Oklahoma: University of Oklahoma Press, 1972.
Hultkrantz, Ake. *The Religions of the American Indians*. Berkeley, Calif.: University of California Press, 1979.
Krickeberg, Walter, *et al. Pre-Columbian American Religions*. New York: Holt, Rinehart and Winston, 1968.
Landes, Ruth. *The Ojibwa Woman*. New York: Ams Press, 1969.
Momaday, Natachee Scott, ed. *American Indian Authors*. Boston: Houghton Mifflin, 1972.
Reichard, Gladys A. *Social Life of the Navaho Indians*. New York: Columbia University Press, 1928.
Sproul, Barbara C., ed. *Primal Myths: Creating the World*. San Francisco: Harper and Row, 1979.
Toelken, Barre. "Seeing with a Native Eye." in *Seeing with a Native Eye*, edited by Walter Holden Capps. New York: Harper & Row, 1976, pp. 9-24.
Underhill, Ruth M. *Red Man's Religion*. Chicago: University of Chicago Press, 1965.
————. *Papago Indian Religion*. New York: Ams Press, 1969.

Chapter 5:
African Religion

Major Concepts of God

We began the previous chapter, "American Indian Religion," with an effort to focus the diversity and unity of the major religious conceptions of the tribes. Assuming a similar nuance here, let us begin with major African concepts of God. Manifestly the many different African tribes have produced many different concepts of God. Nonetheless, convergences and overlappings allow us to speak in general, unifying terms.

Benjamin Ray's *African Religions* distinguishes two major types of divinity. The creator god tended * to be remote and singular, while local gods tended to be close and plural. Two good examples of the creator god are Olorun and Nhialic. Olorun ("Owner of the Sky") was the creator god of the Yoruba, an urbanized people of Nigeria, Dahomey, and Togo. Nhialic ("Above") was the creator god of the Dinka, a pastoral people of southern Sudan.

Yoruba mythology says that Olorun delegated the creation of the world to one of his sons but himself breathed life into human beings and gave each its allotted destiny. Olorun was aloof. The relation between him and the Yoruba was benign but distant. Though humans had separated themselves from

---

*This description is in the past tense because it more surely applies to traditional African belief than to beliefs of today. Still, much of it is valid even in the present.

Olorun by their own fault, this alienation was not the cause of major problems. The myths give several reasons for the separation. One is that humans used to get food from heaven but became greedy, causing Olorun to push the heavens far away. Another is that a woman wiped her dirty hands on heaven and it withdrew. Since Olorun was not responsible for human troubles and did not intervene in history, the Yoruba did not wonder whether he was kind or cruel. Rather, he was universal, impersonal, inactive, silent, and he stimulated no cult. His principal title was "Architect of Destinies," and diviners appealed to him to protect the untainted destiny that he originally set for human beings—protect it from corruption by evil. In times of desperate need, people did appeal to Olorun directly, a fact that qualifies the remoteness he usually had. Moreover, people spiced their conversation with phrases such as "Thanks to Olorun" and "praise to Olorun," while buses and trucks had signs asking Olorun to protect their passengers. Since Olorun normally was beyond the reach of ritual, however, his help was unfathomable.

The Dinka creator god Nhialic created the first human beings and remained their sole creator, shaping them in the womb. Ray calls the relationship between Nhialic and the Dinka oppositional. For instance, a woman hit the sky with her hoe and Nhialic withdrew. "Nhialic became irritated in his heart and hated mankind" (p. 55). Similarly, the first people originally were in darkness, but an ancestor, "Dawn," defied Nhialic and cleaved the earth from the sky so that light could appear. Nhialic throttled Dawn, asking, "Why are you like a man?"

Despite this oppositional relationship, the Dinka wanted Nhialic's personal protection and presence, mainly because he alone could save them from catastrophes. When sickness or death occurred, the Dinka engaged in ritual efforts to reunite the parts of the world affected, so that they might again be in harmony with Nhialic. The original harmony with Nhialic, which the women's hoe broke, was beneficial yet restrictive.

The "fall" from that original harmony was a happy fault. If the Dinka were to have freedom, to live their lives with initiative, they had to break out of the original closeness.

Though Nhialic had no rituals, shrines, priests, or devotees as such, the Dinka said "Nhialic has refused" when they asked other gods (*orisha*) for help and none came. For Nhialic was the ground of all the other gods, divinity as such. All phenomena—rain, fertility, health, the sun—occurred under Nhialic's control and were part of his domain. These phenomena themselves sometimes were deities, but behind them was always Nhialic. Thus Nhialic could be prayed to directly on almost any occasion. "Nhialic, Father, help me!" was a proper Dinka prayer; but whether Nhialic would help or not, no one knew.

The local gods, in contrast to creator gods such as Olorun and Nhialic, were close, active, and many. They symbolized the many facets of religious experience and generated temples, shrines, priests, cults, images, rites, sacrifices, and the like. Thus they were capital in the daily exercise of African religion. A good example of such local gods is the Dinka sky gods. They tended to reveal themselves through possession, causing illness and announcing both their names and their demands. Ajak was a young man living and working in a town. He had left home against his father's will, and the father had died without their being reconciled. Reports Ajak received from home indicated that things were going badly, because the brother who was running them was incompetent. So Ajak was torn between a desire to return home and set things right and a desire to stay in town and keep earning good money.

One night Ajak became possessed. He ran in circles outside his hut, panted heavily, seemed unaware of where he was, fell down, staggered to his feet, sang unintelligible songs, and in general acted very strangely. A priest was summoned. He asked the spirit to tell its name, but he could not compel it. The priest then accused the spirit of wanting a sacrifice (of cattle) that Ajak could not provide, since he was away from home and the family herd. On two other occasions Ajak became possessed, one time nearly plunging into a river infested with crocodiles. Though the spirit possessing him remained unnamed, Ajak developed the theory that it was the god Deng. Probably Deng was offended because Ajak's brother had lost a family cow dedicated to Deng. So Ajak went home and offered sacrifices to Nhialic, his clan gods, and his father's ghost. He and his family smoothed away their differences and his possession-sickness went away.

Yoruba local gods, called *orisha*, also worked through possession. The Yoruba, however, usually desired possession, considering it a way of identifying with the *orisha* personally. Unlike the Dinka, then, the Yoruba worshiped the *orisha* willingly. Usually they worshiped their father's *orisha*, but illness or some other serious problem could suggest that another *orisha* wanted the person as his devotee. A woman who regularly lost her children a few days after birth began one day to make uncontrollable gestures and staggered to the front of Ogun's temple, where she fell stiffly to the ground. This incident was taken to mean that Ogun had chosen her and taken her under his protection. The woman underwent a process of initiation, and three weeks later she appeared at the festival of Ogun ready to be the god's "wife" and serve the people as a medium. Her family expressed their gratitude to the god for choosing her. They recounted the blessings they believed she would receive. Then the festival broadened to include other *orisha*, whose devotees and mediums sang their praises. The whole proceeding resembled a theatrical performance, with costumes, cast, musical accompaniment, and solo and chorus, though the "actors" were normally in a state of trance (Ray, pp. 68-70).

The Ashanti of rural Ghana show another side of the local gods. Called an *obsobom*, the god gave psychiatric advice to clients through priestly mediums. The Ashanti considered the *obsobom* to have full knowledge and authority. They visited his shrine to allay anxieties, give thanks for help they had received, seek cures, and petition for children. If Ashanti petitioners had none of these specific reasons, they could use a general formula: "I am not prospering." Through the priest whom he possessed, the *obsobom* would question the client closely. For instance, a petitioner who came alone would be asked about his wife. When told a wife had refused to come to the shrine, a priest told one client, "She is the cause of your plight. Leave her and take a better woman."

Often Ashanti petitioners blamed economic or social failures on witches or "bad medicine." The *obsobom* priest might well agree, but usually he would not specify the witch or the bad medicine. A normal response was something like, "The cause is among your own kinsmen." Though such a reply was obvious, it took on new authority when it came from the priest of the *obsobom*. For instance, a man who had squandered his wages said that witches had made his hands like sieves. The priest assured him of the *obsobom's* protection against witches but also told him to lock up half his weekly wages in a box. The improvident man did so with alacrity. Similarly, a woman trader who was unable to make a profit in her work was told to go back to farming. Since this advice came from the *obsobom*, she could change her profession without losing face.

The Ashanti tied physical ills to moral defects, as did many other African tribes. Although in recent times the priest would simply advise going to a hospital when the cases were clearly organic, many other cases took the form of "pains all over." They would cause the priest to point to a moral or social cure. Often a general observation such as "You are sick because you are keeping things in your head" would cause the patient to confess what was troubling him: "I have had pains all over since the day I cursed my nephew," or "I have been sick ever since I did my kinsmen out of their share of the cocoa farm." Eating tabooed food, even thinking about using black magic, and ignoring an *obsobom's* advice were other "causes" that the priest's probing might turn up. When they followed the *obsobom*'s advice ("Give a sheep to your nephew," "Give your kinsmen their fair share of the cocoa farm"), the ill Ashanti often were cured speedily. The authority they reposed in the *obsobom* made him a powerful source of personal and social healing.

Authors who stress the influence of local gods can make comparisons across tribes. Despite the plethora of divine functionaries, they usually can find a structural similarity: "The variation in religion has less to do with the ideas themselves than with their expression by means of dissimilar elements linked to the occupations and the floral and fauna of the area" (Zahan, p. 2). Thus the cosmogony of the Dogon has a geometric motif, while that of the Thonga speaks of "issuance from a reed." It seems obvious that these differences reflect the rocky environment of the Dogon, in contrast to the swampy land of the Thonga. For Zahan, the center of the various creation accounts, as of the various cults of local gods, is the situation of human beings in a mysterious universe. To harmonize human beings with their environment, creation myths related them to the inorganic, vegetable, animal, and spiritual realms. Earth, sky, and water were especially important foci. Water tied directly to the possibility of crops and vegetation. Earth and sky once were joined. Their separation (as we saw in the Yoruba and Dinka myths) was necessary for human freedom, and even for communication between humans and God. African rituals based on this separation focused on clouds, rain, and the rainbow, using them as occasions to explain how things were in the beginning. A unique feature of African mysticism was the way God's distance from humans increased their need of him. The distant God procured the purification of human beings and detachment from earthly things. On the other hand, God's distance also provided the intermediate space in which the many local gods functioned. For daily needs the local gods had to suffice.

Even Africans displaced and put upon by recent events

have retained a distant sense of their high God. The modern Ik, the report of whose inhumanity to one another embroiled anthropologist Colin Turnbull in considerable controversy, consider Didigwari too remote now to be of much practical significance. He created them but then retreated into his domain somewhere in the sky, "unreachable and unreaching" (Turnbull, 1972, pp. 184-85). Still, Mount Morungole, where Didigwari first set the Ik on earth, remains a sacred place. "I had noticed this by the almost reverential ways in which they looked at it—none of the shrewd cunning and cold appraisal with which they regard the rest of the world, animate and inanimate. When they talked about it too there was a different quality to their voices, and I found this still to be so long after I had given up expecting anything among the Ik comparable to our notions of what is good and beautiful and truthful" (Turnbull, 1972, p. 187).

Sacrifice and Rites of Passage

The African traditionally responded to God through nature; there were few temples. Rather, believers let nature—the sun, moon, stars, animals, and plants—influence their prayers. Nature was the prime temple—the prime sacred enclosure for worship. The personage who watched over religious relations between the people and either God or the many local gods was the chief: the tribal elder or patriarch. He was both a liaison with the dead and an intermediary between divinity and humanity. For some tribes the chief never really died. He became a quiet animal—for instance, a snake—and joined the ancestors. While living, the chief was responsible for the tribe's prayers and sacrifices, notwithstanding the fact that most tribes also had specialists for these and other religious activities (for example, divination).

For Zahan, sacrifice was the keystone of African traditional religion, the supreme prayer (p. 33). The usual sacrifice was the flowing blood of a slaughtered animal; the blood was thought to unite earth and sky. Normally the victims were domestic animals, who were thought to be part of their human owners, an extension of humanity. The chicken was a popular choice. It was readily available; there were many different kinds of chickens (for the many different kinds of sacrifices); it was easily divided; and it had a relation to time (the rooster greeted the dawn) that gave it cosmic significance. Whatever the animal, though, its blood was valuable as a symbol of life. Spurting forth in sacrifice, blood took life into the invisible, the mystery of life's origin and end.

In the past African royalty who died were often accompanied by other human beings: wives, court officials, relatives, and the like. This practice amounted to human sacrifice. Apparently the victims accepted death willingly, feeling that it was a necessary passageway to fulfillment. This feeling is related to the African tendency to reckon time backward from the ancestors. "Life is born from death and death, in turn, is the prolongation of life" (Zahan, p 45). Among Bushmen tribes of the desert and Hottentots, the elderly accepted such a conception of death by removing themselves to a special hut to die; by so doing they also relieved the tribe of the burden of caring for them. The eldest son would obtain the permission of an old woman to end her misery. The tribe would hold a feast, slaughtering a bull or sheep, and then lead the old woman to the dying-hut.

Not all who died would become "ancestors," however. An ancestor had to be an old, wise person who had not died accidentally or from a disease such as leprosy, who was sound psychologically and physically, morally upright, and an integral member of the tribe. A man or woman with these qualities approached the (almost divine) African ideal, for the tradition by which Africans guided tribal life came from the world of the ancestors. Tradition was the collective wisdom of the tribe, the "word" one found by looking back to the past. This word filled the tribe's prayers, taboos, and rituals. It both derived from the world of the ancestors and gave access to that world. The world of the ancestors was peace, repose, and perfection. Insofar as death, whether normal or sacrificial, swung onto the world of the ancestors and gave one a chance to enter their perfection, it was a friend.

Convictions such as these were assimilated not only through daily living but also in special initiations. These rites nourished the inner personality, which Africans prized more than the outer. Outwardly most Africans appeared exuberant and demonstrative. On long acquaintance, however, observers realized that tribal peoples tended to be close-mouthed about their interior thoughts and slow to correct misinterpretation of their intentions by outsiders. This was a crucial realization, because intention weighed more heavily than outer form or action. For example, it was normal and acceptable for an African to substitute one sacrificial object for another. If the intention was serious and pure whether one sacrificed a bull or a pinch of ash mattered little.

Self-knowledge, focused on interior matters such as intention, was the goal of many initiations. The general African assumption was that persons become human only by stages, and that humanity is a matter of interiority. Becoming human therefore was a progressive movement from the outside to the inside. Initiation might be lifelong, because more interiorization was always possible. Some tribes initiated all males, while others, such as the Dogon, were selective. Women might have initiation ceremonies, or they might be thought to carry knowledge naturally, by virtue of their natural fertility. In the latter case one might find the assimilation of women to nature and men to culture that anthropologists discuss. (See Ortner.)

Initiation encompassed various rites of "passage" from one stage of humanity to a more advanced one. These passages might entail specific knowledge: laws of the body, of cooking, of marital life, of tribal tradition, and so forth. In general one was learning more and more about one's own body and the environment (from which little separated one's own body). The Bantu of Southeast Africa exemplified such initiation well. The first initiation of young Bantu girls, the *khomba*, concerned the laws of the body, the laws of fire, the laws of the hearth, and the laws of cooking. (Each set of laws had a wealth of symbolic and social overtones). The *khomba* took place in the local village. The second initiation, the *tshikanda*, gathered both young women and young men together on a regional basis. It lasted a month and concentrated on the laws of the house, which explained the symbolism of each part of the family residence, and on the categories of the Bantu universe. The third initiation, the *domba*, was conducted on a national level and instructed both young women and young men in the laws of the court. "And since the court is in fact the counterpart of the mythical space of creation, the instruction given to candidates at this initiation, as well as the rites which they perform, refers to their accession to the status of completed persons" (Zahan, p. 56). As completed persons the candidates were ready to marry and give birth to other human beings. They also learned about the drum, which for the Bantu was the creative voice of God.

For many African tribes these initiations entailed considerable pain, the purpose of which was to inculcate self-mastery. Thus from early childhood some tribes disciplined youngsters to a stoic ability to endure pain. For the Fang, this discipline aimed at helping women give birth heedless of labor pains, for the less the mother shouted, the stronger the child would be. For the Dogon, boys had to bear circumsision, and girls excision, without fear or a show of pain. Dogon girls also had to accept rings in their noses, lips, or ears stoically.

Silence was another goal of many initiations. The Dogon considered chattering a serious vice (that is one reason they put rings in the lips of women, whom they considered natural chatterers). Chattering was "speech without a path and without seeds." Bambara girls had their lips tatooed (which turned them violet) to symbolize the "obscurity" that ought to master their speech. The Bambara thought that chatterers brought sickness, death, and the betrayal of secrets, and so both men and women learned from childhood to shun chattering. Bambara games, charades, and symbolic but painful beatings drove home the dangers of a loose tongue. Couples were to keep completely silent during their engagement, for loose talk would imperil their marital unity. Farmers were silent as they sowed their seed, since talking would disperse the care and precision sowing required.

Last, initiations often dramatized the spatial symbolism that many African tribes developed. For instance, they taught candidates the emotional, ritual, and social meanings that the different directions carried. East usually was the direction of life, health, and prosperity. West was the direction of sickness, evil, and death. Thus one faced east while reciting morning prayers or sacrificing at the birth of a child. Left and right sides also carried manifold significance. The left side was likened to females, the west, sunset, water, toads, and the unknown; the right side to males, the east, earth, tortoises, and the known. Therefore the right and left sides of the house had different, complementary overtones.

The Mossi of the Upper Volta were typical in also investing the house with cosmic significance. For them it was a microcosm. With its door and lock, the Mossi hut represented the divinity, a four-faceted being doubly male and female. The hut also symbolized the world—more precisely, the "stomach" of the world. Entering the house was like food entering the stomach; leaving the house was like food being ejected. Finally, the rhythm of work and rest that occurred within the house patterned with the work and rest of nature.

The Dogon had a house-symbolism that was if anything more complex. The *ginna* where the family patriarch resided was an image of the Monitor of the world (a divinity in animal form). The four towers of the *ginna* represented the Monitor's limbs. The kitchen and the stable stood for the Monitor's placenta, and also for its earthly reflection, the head and legs of a man lying on his right side. The workroom stood for the

Monitor's stomach, the two jars of water placed at the entrance of the central room stood for his breasts, and the vestibule stood for his genitals (Zahan, p. 71).

Marcel Griaule, on whose studies of the Dogon Zahan based his interpretation, had the experience (rare for a Westerner) of undergoing a Dogon initiation. He was initiated by Ogotemmeli, a blind Dogon elder. For thirty-three days Ogotemmeli discoursed on different aspects of the Dogon world-view. At the end of this time it was clear that no significant feature of Dogon life was without its celestial archetype and mythic explanation. The granary in which the Dogon stored their food, the drums they beat, their weaving and smithing and threshing—all were sanctioned, accredited, by a heavenly model. Ogotemmeli told Griaule of the jackal, the deluded and deceitful son of God.

> [The jackal] desired to possess speech, and laid hands on the fibres in which language was embodied, that is to say, on his mother's skirt. His mother, the earth, resisted this incestuous action. She buried herself in her own womb, that is to say, in the anthill, disguised as an ant. But the jackal followed her. There was, it should be explained, no other woman in the world whom he could desire. The hole which the earth made in the anthill was never deep enough, and in the end she had to admit defeat. This prefigured the even-handed struggles between men and women, which, however, always end in the victory of the male. The incestuous act was of great consequence. In the first place it endowed the jackal with the gift of speech so that ever afterwards he was able to reveal to diviners the designs of God. (Griaule, p. 21)

Dozens of other vignettes wove an initiation of amazing complexity. Jumping from one symbolic association to another, Ogotemmeli showed his pupil the riches of Dogon imagination. Through generations interiorly minded Dogon had contemplated the shapes, animals, and activities of their world. To explain the origin and function of these things, they had composed vivid stories. That these stories make little

136

sense in modern Western terms is instructive: they are neither science nor history, as modern Westerners understand those terms. Rather, they are religious mythology—stories that prodded the Dogon to contemplate a wonderful nature and life, a reality far too rich for tidy, rational schematization.

Religious Authority Figures

As the stress on initiations suggests, each mature African was supposed to develop religiously—to come to know the tribal traditions and world-view well. This principle did not prevent the rise of religious authority figures, however, whose purpose was to function ritually as mediators between human beings and sacred powers. Let us look briefly at diviners, prophets, priests, and sacred kings.

Diviners who functioned among the Ndembu of northwestern Zambia were basically moral analysts, and they came to their profession only after suffering the afflictions of the divination spirit Kayong'u. In Victor Turner's *Forest of Symbols* the diviner Muchona relates how he became seriously ill when he was thirty-five years old. The only cure turned out to be initiation into the diviner's profession. Muchona was put into a hut and washed with water and medicine. Toward dawn, when the drums began to sound, he was overcome by violent spasms of shaking: Kayong'u had seized him. Attendents marked Muchona's body with red clay, to denote Kayong'u's power to destroy witches. Another playing of the drums, another seizure, and the attendants held out to Muchona a red cock, which signified Kayong'u's awakening. Muchona bit off the head of the cock. The attendants beheaded a goat and Muchona lapped up its blood—another sign of Kayong'u's power in him. Muchona then mounted a clay alligator in which several symbolic objects had been hidden. His ability to divine where they had been placed proved his calling. Thereafter he spent several months learning the lore of basket divination: how to read the pattern of chits mixed in a basket (Ray, pp. 103-4).

The basic task of the Ndembu diviner was to disclose the causes of misfortune and death. Doing this entailed scrutiny, not of the future, but of the past, to identify the spiritual and human agents that caused the misfortune or death. "Since all human problems, such as infertility, illness, and trouble in hunting, are ascribed to moral conflicts within the human community, the diviner's task is to disclose acts of immorality that have provoked the vengeance of the ancestors and to reveal the destructive hand of witches and sorcerers" (Ray, p. 104). The diviner would rigorously interrogate the parties to a case. Through this interrogation he developed a "map" of the social relationships involved that enabled him to estimate who was likely to be responsible for the death or sickness. Then, entering trance, the diviner would be taken over by Koyong'u and would sift out the truth from the falsehood in the case, using his winnowing basket. Each chit in the basket was a symbolic counter for some sort of misfortune, social relationship, or malicious motivation. Ndembu diviners saw themselves as moral analysts of the tribe's behavior, and their diagnoses aimed at restoring approved morality. Since much Ndembu illness and misfortune was psychosomatic, the diviner could be quite successful in curing and consoling.

A different sort of divination occurred among the Yoruba, who were more interested in the future. The Yoruba believe in predestination, and their diviner was called *babalawo* ("Father of secrets"), because of his ability to reveal a client's destiny. This ability might be inherited, or it might derive from being chosen by Orunmila, the god of divination. Either way it required an apprenticeship of ten or twelve years, during which the candidate had to learn a prodigious amount of Yoruba lore, poetry, and the like. This lore formed the basis of a divination process involving sixteen palm nuts. The pattern that the nuts formed when shaken and rolled out was the basis for determining the client's future. The different poems at the diviner's disposal expressed the various anxieties of Yoruba life. The client would keep his exact problem secret, so that the diviner could express only the god's objective declaration. In effect, then, the Yoruba divination was like a Rorschach test, in which subjective interpretation (of the god's declaration) by the client was all important.

African *prophets* took more initiative than diviners, going to the people to inspire religious and political movements. They also tended to speak the divine word directly, bypassing symbolic media such as divination baskets and palm nuts. Nuer prophets active in the southern Sudan exemplified this aspect of African religion. "They organized cattle raids against the Dinka, performed rituals to stem widespread epidemics, and introduced new divinities from neighboring societies. Later they led resistance movements against Arab slavers and British colonial powers" (Ray, p. 111).

According to Evans-Pritchard, the first Nuer prophet of note was Ngundeng, a prophet of the spirit *deng,* who died in 1906. Ngundeng obtained his powers by prolonged fasting and unusual abnegations. "It is said that he lived for weeks by himself in the bush, eating animal and human excrement, that he used to sit on a cattle pen in his kraal [enclosure] and let it penetrate his anus, that he used to wander about the bush for days mumbling to himself or sit in his cattle byre doing the same, and that when in such a mood he would refuse food except ashes, which he had cooked for him" (p. 305). Ngundeng had a great mound built to honor *deng* that became a cultic center for all of Nuerland. (The British blew it up in 1928.)

Out of such bizarre behavior as Ngundeng's, Nuer prophets derived inspiration from a possessing spirit, whose mouthpiece they became. Their most influential function was mediating directions for warfare. "They spoke the directions of the spirits of the air for raids on the Dinka and for resistance to the slavers and the administration and made sacrifices to them. Their other functions were subsidiary and were exercised by lesser prophets also: healing, particularly curing barrenness of women, staying of epidemics lethal to men or cattle, and exorcism of troublesome spirits. They were also credited with power to foretell events and with a more than usual insight" (Evans-Pritchard, p. 308).

Prophecy was not a traditional Nuer institution. It arose because of social pressures—threats to the established way of life that required an organ of protest and opposition. The same dynamics appeared in recent prophecy among the Lugbara of northwest Uganda. In the late nineteenth century Arabs and Europeans intruded upon the Lugbara, as did slave raiding, ivory raiding, and epidemics of rinderpest (a cattle disease) and meningitis. Under the leadership of the prophet Rembe, the Lugbara responded with the Yakan water cult.

Rembe brought sacred water from the southern Sudan, and from those to whom he sold it he formed a new, intertribal organization. This new tribal system successfully opposed German troops, then took the lead in opposing the Belgian administration of the area. There was a pause when the Belgians withdrew, but when the British took over in 1914, the Yakan (as the water-group were called) mobilized again. Using an outbreak of meningitis, smallpox, and influenza as a divine sign that the British were poisonous, the Yakan, led by Rembe, traveled the country dispensing sacred water: the water would protect the Lugbara from rifle bullets and epidemics. Many Ugandans rallied to Rembe, gave over their traditional feuds, and forged a new national consciousness. Though the British authorities finally crushed the movement and deported the Yakan leaders, Rembe achieved high status as a "man of God." The Lugbara saw him as an emissary of Adro, the creator, who was re-creating their world. They hoped that from the anarchy they were experiencing, which resembled the fertile time of the original creation, a new social order might emerge (Ray, pp. 113-15).

African *priests* tended to concern themselves with ritual and symbolic matters. If the prophet expressed the people's fears and hopes, the priest expressed its community life. "Though it is sometimes misleading to distinguish sharply between 'priest' and 'prophet,' the distinctive mark of a prophet is his inspired sociopolitical leadership, while the distinctive mark of a priest is his ritual and symbolic authority. The main task of a priest is to sustain and renew the life of the community he serves. Often the priest contains within himself the life-force which he seeks to mediate to his people" (Ray. p. 116).

For the Dinka of East Africa, the god Longar gave the divinity Flesh to priests as a source of life-giving power. The priests were masters of fishing-spears, which symbolized this power, and Flesh was the source of the light by which the priests illumined the world. The priests' knowledge and vision made them the "lamps" of the Dinka, and their words changed sacrificial situations from suffering and death to life and renewal. In wielding the symbolic spear ritually, the priests repeated the archetypal work of Longar, who once led the starving Dinka to green pastures. They released the life-force from the sacrificial victim, so that it could benefit the Dinka community.

This close connection with the life-force gave the Dinka priest a special death-ritual. When spearmasters were about to die, they asked the people to bury them alive. The spearmaster would sit in his grave and speak his last words to the people. They then would cover his grave with cattle dung. The people would not mourn, and no one would say that the master had died. Rather, the people would rejoice with songs, saying that the master had been taken from the earth for their good. In effect they believed that the master's life continued on among them (Ray, pp. 116-17).

Among the Dogon a priest-chief called a Hogon was the head of both a council of elders and a line of totemic priests. Symbolically he represented the original ancestors and the original cosmic seeds. Because both the ancestors and the seeds had other relations (the Dogon mythology, as previously mentioned, was especially complex), the Hogon came to center all of Dogon reality. "The Hogon thus unites in himself the social, ecological, and cosmic order, and as such he is the personification of the total universe" (Ray, p. 118). His priestly mediation was less a series of ritualistic acts than an ongoing dramaturgy: the totality of the Hogon's apparel, household, and daily activities evoked the Dogon universe. He would rise at dawn and face the east; at sunset he would sit down and face the west. His actions during the planting, growing, and dry seasons were similarly symbolic, for the Hogon controlled—or at least seriously influenced—the rhythms of nature and mediated nature's generative power.

The last African religious authority figure to be considered is the *sacred king*. At one time it was fashionable to link this figure with the sacred kings of Egypt, arguing that Egyptian customs traveled south and shaped the kingship of tribes below the Sahara. Today this theory is out of fashion, for historians believe they can account for sub-Sahara sacral kingship on indigenous grounds. One such ground might have been the need for a central leadership for ventures of military conquest.

Since in past decades the killing of the king of the Shilluk, a tribe of East Africa, received the attention of distinguished anthropologists such as James G. Frazier and E. E. Evans-Pritchard, it appears in most discussions of African sacred kingship today. The king of Shilluk was a ritual figure, a political figure, and the incarnation of the hero-divinity Nyikang, who symbolized Shilluk national identity. In the king's installation the people ritualized their need to unify opposing political factions and also to bring together both the political and the religious dimensions of their lives. Scholars debate precisely how much regicide actually occurred among the Shilluk, but insofar as the Shilluk did kill kings who had become feeble or who had become identified with sectional interests and no longer served national unity, they brought to its logical conclusion a sense that the king had to focus the entire people—its vigor, national unity, welfare, and good relations with the sacred. This interpretation is bolstered by the fact that the Shilluk king actually governed very little. He was the supreme judge and final appeal in cases of homicide, theft, incest, and crimes that threatened the foundations of Shilluk political and social order, but his day-to-day work was meager. His main reason for being was symbolic.

The king of the Swazi of southeastern Africa also was both the ritual and the political head of his nation, but there were even stronger *cosmic* overtones to his rule. These were clearly expressed in a ceremony (the *Ncwala*) that occurred annually at the winter solstice. At that time, the Swazi thought, the king's powers had declined to their lowest point and needed renewal. The *Ncwala* therefore was rich in symbols of breaking with the old and starting anew. The people would sing that they hated the king and rejected him. He would spit sacred medicine to the east and west to destroy the old year. Then young warriors would bring green branches to the king, that he might be reborn—revitalized. The warriors would chase a black bull, pummel the life out of it, and make the king a strong medicine from pieces of the bull. The king himself would mount another bull and be washed with foaming water to renew his virility.

As the ceremony continued through several other symbolic actions, the byplay between old weakness and new virility riveted attention to the liminality, the transitoriness, of the period that both the cosmos and the kingdom were in. Toward the climax of these liminality symbols the king would appear as *Silo*, a weird personification of nature forces, and perform a jerky, frightening dance of power and pain. Entering into his new fullness of power, he would cohabit with his chief queen, then stay in seclusion from the people, for his force had become too potent for them to bear. When he finally reappeared, he would be cleansed and put the "dirt" of the old year conclusively to rest. "At the end of the *Ncwala* there is a feeling of general well-being as the rain falls and the people taste of their newly harvested crops. Once again the king and the nation are strong" (Ray, p. 124).

The king most dramatically focused Africa's sense of the

cosmological myth, but the other religious authority figures also were concerned with mediating fertility and sacral power. The Dinka priest-master of the fishing-spear, for instance, presided over a sacrifice that transmuted death-force into life-force. So too the diviners and prophets focused a cosmological orientation, for the patterns they discerned and the gods they spoke for were immanent to nature, not transcendent. Thus African archaic religion verified the description we developed when treating "yesterday." Fertility, world-influencing spirits, and an effort to harmonize with nature shaped all the traditional tribes.

Case Study: An Aged Contemporary Pygmy

During the 1950s the British anthropologist Colin Turnbull lived for several years with a group of BaMbuti—Pygmies of the Ituri Forest in what was then the Belgian Congo. His account of these years, *The Forest People,* is a remarkable rendition of the Pygmies' life. Individual personalities emerge, there is little tedious analysis or jargon, and the reader comes away with an immense appreciation of the Pygmies' humanity.

In terms of its economy and social structure the Pygmies' existence in the forest was very simple. The tribe was small scale: at the level of hunting and gathering. But the Pygmies' life in and with the forest was also a fine example of archaic ecology. When Turnbull took Kenge, his closest Pygmy friend and best informant, out of the Ituri forest to the Ruwenzori Mountains of Uganda, Kenge literally could not see things in perspective. He had become so accustomed to the shortened vistas the forest imposed that he could not see animals grazing a mile away. To him they were only little bugs or dots. The concept of correcting for distance was completely foreign to him. The forest's short range dominated Kenge's very optical nerves.

In later studies of the Ik, a mountain people who lived along the border of Kenya and Uganda, Turnbull found the reverse of this ecology. Denied the right to follow their herds, the Ik became maladapted to the land. Hunger, malnutrition, and social breakdown followed. Indeed, by the time Turnbull came to live with them, the Ik had become a horrible tribe, giving flesh to Hobbes's dictum that "human beings treat one another like wolves." The BaMbuti, fortunately, suffered no such displacement from their traditional habitat. Through the 1950s they continued to enjoy the forest as a benevolent home. The interviews that Turnbull had with the aged Pygmy Moke brought the depth of this symbiosis home. Near the end of his years, Moke was a repository of Pygmy wisdom. If we listen to his meditative explanations of Pygmy belief with an inner ear, we can catch undertones of the religion that a fortunate, happy archaic existence nurtured.

Turnbull had discerned that the central ceremony and mystery of Pygmy life was the *molimo*. This was a ceremony involving choral responses between the Pygmies and a hauntingly beautiful tubal sound that hovered at the edge of the campfire circle. The *molimo* was both this choral ceremony and the source of the tubal sound. The Pygmies implied that the source was something alive—a god or animal or living force—but they were unabashed when Turnbull later discovered that the *molimo* was actually a long piece of metal tubing. That was insignificant; what was important was the ceremony's meaning, its reason and cause. Though the *molimo* was informal, it mesmerized the Pygmies; night after night they spent inordinate amounts of time on it. Moke decided to enlighten Turnbull about this, because he judged that the time had come when Turnbull was ready to look at the inside of Pygmy existence.

Moke's explanation took the form of a muttering commentary, carried out while he whittled a bow. Turnbull was the addressee, but only indirectly, for the old man was also speaking to himself. Bemused, ruminative, he began by noting that the Pygmies called out the *molimo* when things began going wrong. "It may be that the hunting is bad . . . or that someone is ill, or, as now, that someone has died. These are not good things, and we like things to be good. So we call out the *molimo* and it makes them good, as they should be" (Turnbull, 1962, p. 91). How did the molimo do that? By awakening the forest, in whose goodness the Pygmies placed their faith.

As Moke described it, the forest was both father and mother to the Pygmies. It gave them everything they needed: food, clothing, shelter, warmth, and affection. Because of this provision, things normally went well; usually the children prospered from the parents' care. So when things went wrong, there had to be a reason. The simplest reason was that the forest was sleeping, and therefore the *molimo* was the Pygmies' effort to awaken the forest. They sang as beautifully as they could so that the forest would awaken happy.

Turnbull was deeply moved by this innocent, trusting view. It was touching in itself, but all the more so when contrasted with the views of the tribes that bordered the Pygmies. For those village people times of crisis meant they had been cursed by an evil spirit or a witch. The Pygmies' world was kinder, simpler, more down to earth. By analogy with their own reactions they knew that the forest would not allow them to be harmed if it were awake. "Normally everything goes well in our world. But at night when we are sleeping, sometimes things go wrong, because we are not awake to stop them from going wrong. Army ants invade the camp; leopards may come in and steal a hunting dog or even a child. If we were awake these thing would not happen" (*ibid.,* p. 92).

By analogy, then, something big gone wrong meant that the forest was sleeping. If the Pygmies could awaken it sweetly, surely it would quickly resume its care of them. Then everything would be well again. Still, that everything became well again would not mean the end of the *molimo.* As Moke ruminated on, it became clear that the *molimo* was not just for times of crisis, it was for times of plenty and joy as well. "So when our world is going well then also we sing to the forest because we want it to share our happiness" (*ibid.*).

Turnbull had heard parts of this explanation before, but Moke's instruction made it all fall into place. The *molimo* was a nightly chorus of communion, an intimate exchange, between the Pygmies and their god. Moke made this "theology" explicit. Smiling, he turned his wrinkled old face and deep brown eyes to Turnbull and said that although all Pygmies have different names for their god, they all know that it is really the same one. Just what god is, of course, no one knows. That is why the name doesn't matter very much. "How can we know? . . . We can't see him; perhaps only when we die will we know and then we can't tell anyone. So how can we say what he is like or what his name is? But he must be good to give us so many things. He must be of the forest. So when we sing, we sing to the forest" (*ibid.*, pp. 92-93).

The Pygmies believed so much in the forest's goodness that they seldom asked for particular boons. It was not necessary to ask that the hunt go better, or that someone's illness be cured. It was enough to awaken the forest. The forest would take care. The most the Pygmies would do, when hard times were prolonged, was to sing songs of special devotion and praise—to try especially hard to awaken the forest sweetly. In one song they would sing: "There is darkness all around us; but if darkness *is*, and the darkness is of the forest, then the darkness must be good" (*ibid.*, p 93)

Moke was an old man, whose faith in the forest had become simplified over many years. No doubt younger Pygmies suffered more doubts, at least from time to time. Though life in the forest was relatively easy, there were frictions, misfortunes, and occasional hard times. The Pygmies were human, and so they knew fools and knaves. But the inner pulse of their culture, the meaning to which they finally turned again and again, very likely did have a great resemblance to Moke's trust in the forest, for all the Pygmies thought of themselves as "the forest people." None of them ever left the forest without desiring to return quickly. It was the site of their god, the place where things felt right.

In too many anthropological studies, and too many studies by historians of religion, the reader drowns in details. Impressed by the complexity of an archaic culture, by its manysided symbolism, the writer tries to render the lush whole. This practice has obvious benefits, but also serious drawbacks. As the price of their luxurious description, many studies miss the simple core. To be sure, simplicity can be deceptive. "Seek simplicity and distrust it," many methodologists repeat. But simplicity at least befits old age, because old age is apt for wisdom. In the forest or the city, wisdom orders the many into one.

It may be that a Western anthropologist, no matter how *sympatico* with African natives, or how trusted, gives us native wisdom dubiously. It may also be that when we find indications of a divine unity and goodness we have loved from our own beginning, we respond excessively. Nonetheless, there *are* privileged moments of understanding, even across great cultural chasms. As in friendship, creative intuition, or deep prayer, there are scholarly times when one "knows," without complexity or doubt. By luck or grace or the alignment of the planets, the turning world has shown its still point. Then there can be communion, colloquy heart to heart.

Speaking from the heart, Moke touched Turnbull deeply. Speaking from the heart, Turnbull touched me deeply. Among all the rough and rugged rocks of "higher" religions and theologies, I have found no better description of a gracious divinity, or a wholehearted faith, then this confession of a naked little man, less than four feet tall, whose eyes glistened as he whittled his bow. Down fifteen feet of a drain pipe, a *molimo* in modern garb, he and his fellow Pygmies nightly sang songs to god. *"Bis orat qui cantat,"* Augustine opined: "she who sings prays twice." Deep in the forest some little people who sang the molimo probably prayed three times.

Bibliography

Evans-Pritchard, E. E. *Nuer Religion*. New York: Oxford University Press, 1977.
Griaule, Marcel. *Conversations with Ogotemmeli*. New York: Oxford University Press, 1965.
King, Noel Q. *Religions of Africa*. New York: Harper & Row, 1970.
Mbiti, John S. *African Religions and Philosophy*. New York: Doubleday, 1970.
Merriam, Alan P. *An African World*. Bloomington, Ill.: Indiana University Press, 1974.
Mertens, Alice and Brosler, Joan. *African Elegance*. Cape Town, South Africa: Purnell, 1973.
Mitchell, Robert Cameron. *African Primal Religions*. Niles, Ill.: Argus, 1977.
Ortner, Sherry B. "Is Female to Male as Nature Is to Culture." in *Woman, Culture & Society*. edited by M. Z. Rosaldo and L. Lamphere. Stanford, Calif.: Stanford University Press, 1974
Parrinder, Geoffrey. *African Mythology*. London: Paul Hamlyn, 1967.
————.*African Traditional Religion*. 3d. ed. New York: Harper & Row, 1976.
Ranger, T. O. and Kimambo, I. N., eds. *The Historical Study of African Religion*. Berkley, Calif.: University of California Press, 1972.
Ray, Benjamin C. *African Religions*. Englewood Cliffs, N.J.: Prentice Hall, 1976.
Turnbull, Colin. *The Forest People*. New York: Simon & Schuster, 1963.
————.*The Mountain People*. New York: Simon & Schuster, 1972.
————,ed. *Africa and Change*. New York: Alfred A. Knopf, 1973.
Turner, Victor. *Forest of Symbols*. Ithaca, N.Y.: Cornell University Press, 1967.
Werber, R. P. *Regional Cults*. London: Academic Press, 1977.
Zahan, Dominique. *The Religion, Spirituality, and Thought of Traditional Africa*. Chicago: University of Chicago Press, 1979.

Chapter 6:
Australian Religion

The Australian Mythic World

Prehistoric peoples, peoples of early civilizations, peoples of the world religions, American Indians, and Africans all developed rich mythologies. Through storied explanations of the world's origin and build, they related to the cosmos with meaning and dignity. The mythology of archaic Australians was a match for any of these other peoples'.

Aboriginal Australian mythology reflected a millennial accumulation of knowledge and experience. It was the dominant force in traditional daily life, paradoxically because of its "eternity." The stories that Australians learned were authoritative because they came from the more real world of the divine ancestors—the culture heroes who were the source of sacred ritual power. The ancestors were actors in eternal, authoritative myths. Thus when archaic Australians performed a mytho-ritualistic ceremony, they released power from the eternal ancestors that caused the seasonal cycles, the growth of the animals, and human and plant fertility (Berndt, 1963, pp. 53-54).

The general Australian conception of creation was that in the beginning land and sea existed, but they were unformed and unmoving. The eternal ancestors of the dreamtime awoke and took long journeys over the land. As they journeyed they created the plants and animals, rivers and waterholes, stars and clouds, hills and islands. They created by traveling, hunting, camping, making love, and fighting, and they often took the form of their creations. As the peak of their creation the eternal ancestors created the Dark Australians, placing them in the midst of the beautiful land to love it. Then the eternal ancestors disappeared into the land, leaving traces on rocks, waterholes, rivers, and caves for the Dark People to wonder about.

By transforming themselves into their creation and leaving these traces, the ancestors gave the aborigines the totems that focused their religion. Everything in the traditional Australian world owed its explanation to the ancestors, and the totems—emblems of their presence—grounded the whole system. Both the natural landscape and the mores of the archaic peoples derived from the ancestors. Both their ecology and their sociology moved in tandem with the dreamtime of creation that the myths described. For example, through a totem such as the kangaroo archaic Australians would explain the origin of their own spirit or their clan; the kangaroo stood for the ancestor who created them. Aborigines traditionally believed that each person's spirit came from a clan pool. It then entered the mother's womb, but at death it would return to the clan pool. The totem that marked his clan determined most of an Australian's social relationships: whom he could marry, how his children would fit into the tribe, how he ought to conduct himself toward other tribal members. The eternal ancestors had sanctioned this subdivision of the Dark People into their various totemic groups.

To return to the ancestors, the archaic Australians enacted a great cycle of initiation ceremonies, which they held at places in the landscape that the ancestors had marked. The ceremonies re-enacted events of the creative dreamtime. Chanting, dancing, and acting out the creation-drama, the Australian would "become" the ancestor he represented. The ceremonies were so sacred, so vital to tribal life, that those excluded from particular ones were excluded under pain of death (women and uninitiated boys were excluded from the sort we are considering here). For unless the creational cycle were reenacted purely, cosmic life would not continue. It was only the creational force of the ancestors, available in the constant "now" of the eternal dreamtime, that kept the world in existence.

Dreamtime therefore contained past, present, and future in one. Most likely this comprehensive, rather sophisticated conception evolved only over long periods of time. In fact, the ritual language of some tribes was so archaic that it was comprehensible only to the old men of the tribe, who had to translate it for the others. The dreamtime of creation was also the Golden Age, when all the rivers were full and the land was totally beautiful. Golden Ages are common in religious mythology—so common that interpreters automatically take them as projections of a people's sense of what ought to be, of the perfect existence they intuited but never realized. Usually, however, the Golden Age of creation lies in the past, separated from the present by a "fall." The Genesis account of human creation—Adam and Eve, and the garden of paradise—is a good example. It is striking, therefore, that the Australian Golden Age continued to be available in the present. Eternal and outside human time, it could be called up from any given human moment. By "dreaming"—mythic imagination—the archaic Australian could become contemporary with a creative force always in existence (Baglin and Moore, pp. 23-27).

With this orientation to archaic Australian religious culture, we can pause to sketch something of the history and physical features of the tribes. In terms of evolutionary history the aborigines represent an archaic form of the Caucasoid race. The different tribes are quite homogeneous, a fact that argues that they come from a common stock. Radiocarbon datings suggest that they had come to Australia by 30,000 B.E.C., which would have been during the final glaciation of the Pleistocene Era. Where they came from remains disputed, but Indonesia is a strong likelihood. Economically the tribes never progressed beyond hunting and gathering. A likely reason is that there were no indigenous plants or animals suitable for domestication. Before contact with Europeans, the aborigines probably numbered about 300,000, divided into some seven hundred tribes (many of them speaking different dialects). They lived nomadic lives, hunting, gathering, and fishing, unless they happened to inhabit an area especially rich in food sources.

The nomadic tribes traveled light. Both sexes wore little or no clothing; their instruments for hunting, gathering, and defense were little more than a spear, a stone axe, a shield, and a boomerang; their other possessions were limited to a dillybag (a mesh bag of fibers with a drawstring), a digging stick, and a wooden dish. Some tribes built large shelters, to which they would return regularly. Men hunted the large game, fished with spears, did deep-sea fishing with lines, and cooked on open fires. Women gathered seeds, fruits, roots, small marsupials, shellfish, and reptiles, and fished with lines. Women would grind their seeds and nuts into cakes, which they baked in ashes. Both sexes decorated themselves, using headbands, earrings, nosepegs, and colorings for the hair and face. They also cut cicatrices (wounds that scar) into the chest, back, stomach, and thighs.

Archaic Australian law and government depended on clan organization and therefore on the mythology of the dream-time. Men were the tribal leaders, and they had a strict rank, correlated with their ritual standing. To break tribal customs (for example, to elope in order to marry a tabooed spouse) usually meant death—one was violating an eternal order. (If the eloping couple could get far away from their own clan and be received into another clan, they might survive.) The medicine man, whom we shall study in the next section, was so important a figure that he stood outside the normal clan structure.

Feuds between tribes were frequent, though sometimes they were resolved by ceremonial battles. Then able-bodied men of both sides would line up facing one another with their spears and boomerangs. With the women and children looking on and cheering, they would let these weapons fly at one another. Honor was satisfied and reconciliation ceremonies could begin as soon as blood was drawn. At times ceremonial warfare was reduced to a contest between one tribe's champion and the other's (Baglin and Moore, p. 64).

Having considered some main features of archaic Australian mythology and physical life, let us now consider the mythology of two specific tribes, the Aranda and the Kakadu. Both were greatly interested in human fertility, the Aranda paying more attention to the masculine side, and the Kakadu to the feminine.

The Aranda myth of Kakora made him a Great Father. In the beginning everything was resting in perpetual darkness, and Kakora was sleeping in everlasting night. Kakora began thinking, and desires flashed through his mind. Bandicoots (small marsupials) began to come out of his navel and armpits. Kakora rose up from under the earth, saw that the sun was shining, and felt dazed and hungry. He seized two bandicoots, cooked them in white-hot soil heated by the sun, and ate them. Then he began looking for a mate, but it was getting dark and he found none before he fell asleep. While he was asleep, something emerged from under his armpit in the shape of a bull-roarer (wooden pieces that, when twirled, produce a roaring noise). It took a human form and became Kakora's first-born son.

Upon awakening, Kakora stirred his son to life by making a loud, vibrating call (with the bull-roarer?). The son rose up and danced a ceremonial dance around his father, who was sitting adorned with full ceremonial designs worked in blood and feather-down. That evening two more sons were born from Kakora's armpits. During the day they hunted, and at night more sons were born. This pattern went on for many days. After numerous adventures Kakora returned to his eternal sleep under the earth. Australians may visit him, for he lies under the present-day Ilbalintja Soak (a spring). The myth gives the conditions for a good visit: "Men and women who approach the soak to quench their thirst may do so only if they bear in their hands bunches of green inuruna boughs which they lay down on the edge of the soak. For then Kakora is pleased with their coming and smiles in his sleep" (Sproul, pp. 321-23).

The Ilbalintja Soak functioned for the Aranda as a totemic place, and the myth of Kakora's first sons' dance, over which Kakora presided in ceremonial garb, gave a warrant and paradigm for an Aranda fertility ceremony using blood and feather-down. Socially the Aranda were heavily dominated by males, a fact that perhaps explains the myth's male parthenogenesis (procreation without heterosexual union).

Kakadu mythology featured Imberombera, the Great Mother. She had a giant consort, Wuraka, but he was fatigued by his potency and longed only to rest. At that time there were no black Australians. Imberombera wanted Wuraka to travel with her, but he was too tired (his penis was too heavy), and so he sat down (a great rock arose to mark the place). Imberombera carried many children in her huge stomach. On her head was a bamboo ring from which hung many dillybags full of yams. Imberombera left many boy and girl spirit children at a place called Marpur. She told them to speak Iwaidja and to eat the yams she left behind. Imberombera then traveled to many other places, leaving yams and spirit children. At Mamul she told the children to speak Umoriu, and at ten other places she left children and instructed them to speak different languages. Imberombera therefore functioned for the Kakadu as a several-sided fertility source. Children, plants, and languages all derived from her actions in the dreamtime. It is tempting to speculate that the Kakadu mythology expressed a memory that women were responsible not only for children but also for discovering edible plants and fostering culture (Sproul, pp. 323-25).

Fertility also dominated the myths of the Wulamba, who

lived on the northern tip of the continent. In dreamtime their eternal ancestors Djanggawul and his two sisters roamed the earth, creating plants, animals, and sacred objects. They brought sacred fertility objects from the realm of not-being: the ngainmara mat that symbolized the womb and the rangga poles that symbolized the phallus. These three ancestors created equally until the sisters left their sacred paraphernalia unguarded and Djanggawul stole them. With this symbol, as well as with the symbol of Djanggawul shortening his sisters' clitorises, the Wulamba expressed their sense that early on a revolution from original sexual equality to male rule had occurred. The creation activities of the three ancestors, and their sexual activities, became the basis for much Wulamba ritual (Sproul, p. 315).

The Australian Medicine Man

The central religious authority figure in archaic Australian religion was the medicine man, who basically fitted a shamanic mold. He cured the sick, defended the community against black magic, discovered those responsible for premature deaths, and played an important role in the initiation ceremonies. The medicine man derived his status and power from his special relation with the ancestors. Whereas all Australians could return to the creative period through "dreaming," the medicine man was thought actually to be able to recover the ancestors' condition. Thus he was thought to be able to fly and ascend to heaven, to descend to the underground, to talk with the ancestors, and to see spirits. The usual way for the medicine man to obtain these powers was through an initiatory death and resurrection. The candidate was "killed," magical substances were placed in his body (which substances became like new, supernatural organs), and then he returned to life.

Among the Aranda the medicine man could be initiated by spirits or by other medicine men. If the spirits were to initiate him, he would go to sleep at the mouth of a cave. A spirit would come and throw an invisible lance at him that would pierce his neck from behind, pass through his tongue (making a large hole), and then come out through his mouth. (Proof that this happened was the hole in the candidate's tongue after his initiation. Usually it was big enough to pass one's little finger through.) Then a second lance would cut off the candidate's head and he would die. The spirit would take him deep into the cave, where there was perpetual light and cool springs (the Aranda notion of paradise). There the spirit would tear out the candidate's internal organs and give him new ones. The candidate would return to life but for some time would behave like a lunatic. The spirit would carry him back to camp (since the spirit was invisible, no one would see him do this except other medicine men), where the candidate had to wait a year before he could begin to practice. If the opening in his tongue closed during that time, he would have to give up his vocation, for that would be a sign that his mystical powers had disappeared. During the year he would study with other medicine men, concentrating especially on the uses of the new organs that the spirit had placed in his body.

When the medicine man was initiated by other medicine men, his death-resurrection included a ritual operation. Two old medicine men would rub his body with rock crystals, abrading the skin. They would press rock crystals into his scalp, pierce a hole under a fingernail of his right hand, and make an incision in his tongue. Then they would mark his forehead with a design known as "the devil's hand," and mark his body with another design representing the spirits and the magical crystals (Eliade, pp. 146-47).

Since the medicine man, whose initiation was similar in all tribes, had died and been reborn, he could live between the two worlds, mediating between the eternal ancestors and his earthly fellow-humans. This mediatorship functioned in many ways. The medicine man was a more powerful dreamer than the ordinary Australian, and so he could create new rituals based on his special access to the realities of eternal dreamtime. He could cure the sick by seeing the magical objects that were causing their illness. He could make rain by flying to the heavens and defend his tribe by singing poison into its enemies. Among the Wiradjuri, a strong medicine man could revive a dead person if she had been spiritually strong. In many tribes the medicine man was the intellectual, the repository of tribal lore. Usually he led the totemic ceremonies, and often he was also the temporal chief. Always his opinion carried great prestige.

From an account of the initiation of a Wiradjuri medicine man we can get a sense of the relation to a particular eternal ancestor that a medicine man might have. Since the Wiradjuri allowed medicine men to inherit their profession, the candidate in this account was initiated by his father. The father began the ceremony by evoking a rapture to transform the son's life. This he did by taking the son into the bush and placing two large quartz crystals against his breast. They vanished into his body, where he felt them going through him like warmth. The father gave the boy other crystals, which looked like ice and tasted like sweet water. Following this experience in the bush, the boy could see ghosts.

After his tooth-removal ceremony, which advanced him toward manhood, the boy saw his father go down into the ground and come up covered with red dust. The father asked the boy to bring up a piece of crystal from his body, and the boy was able to do so. Then the father led the boy through a hole in the ground to a grave. Inside the grave a dead man rubbed the boy all over, to make him clever, and gave him some crystals. As the father and son emerged from the grave they saw a tiger snake. The father explained that the snake would be the boy's totem, as it had been his own. A string was tied to the snake's tail. The father took hold of the string, and they followed the snake. They went into the ground, came up inside a hollow tree, and met many other snakes that rubbed themselves against the boy, again to make him clever.

The climax of the initiation was a trip to the ancestor Baiame. Astride more strings, the father and son were flown by Wombu, Baiame's bird, through the clouds to the other side of the sky. There they went through the door that healers go through, on the other side of which they saw Baiame sitting in his camp. He was a very old man with a long beard. He sat with his legs under him and two great quartz crystals extended from his shoulders to the sky above. Surrounding Baiame were his people, who were birds and beasts (Eliade, pp. 131-32).

Several details in this account reflect typically shamanic themes. The flight to Baiame fits the pattern of "magical flight" that shamans of many different cultures reveal. The ecstasy in which shamans specialized was more often than not a release of the spirit toward "heaven," where dwelt the higher forces with whom the shaman communed. Other Australian accounts develop the notion of the strings by which the Wiradjuri boy and his father followed the totemic snake and were flown to heaven by Wombu, Baiame's bird. The medicine men either projected these strings from their bodies or extended them from their hair. Alternative means of flight were nose-bones that the spirits could grasp to pull the medicine men through the sky, or transformation into birds. Thus the medicine men of the Kurnai wore a nose-bone, while the Aranda medicine men became eagle-hawks. Kimberley medicine men favored the string motif, visiting the dead by ascending a string. During initiations in the Forest River District, older medicine men would carry the initiate to Ungud, the rainbow serpent, by a string that hung from the sky and had crosspieces on which two men could sit (Eliade, pp. 138-40).

It is interesting that the best-selling American shamanism of recent times, that described by Carlos Castaneda in his several books, also dealt with lines of force. The shamanism that Castaneda described (or made up) derived from Yaqui Indian lore, and it involved tapping the *nagual*, an impersonal energy field. Nonetheless, its use of strings for flight was remarkably similar to the Australian shaman's:

> Don Genaro adopted a strange dancing posture. His knees were bent, his arms were extended to his sides, his fingers outstretched. He seemed to be about to twirl; in fact, he half whirled around and then he was pulled up. I had the clear perception that he had been hoisted up by a line of a giant caterpillar that lifted his body to the very top of the cliff. My perception of the upward movement was a most weird mixture of visual and bodily sensations. I half saw and half felt his flight to the top. There was something that looked or felt like a line or an almost imperceptible thread of light pulling him up. . . . Don Genaro repeated his feat three more times. Each time, my perception was tuned. During his last upward leap I could actually distinguish a series of lines emanating from his midsection, and I knew when he was about to ascend or descend, judging by the way the lines of his body moved. When he was about to leap upward, the lines bent upward; the opposite happened when he was about to leap downward; the lines bent outward and down. (Castaneda, pp. 220-21)

Whether he actually experienced these things or contrived them through literary imagination, Castaneda has offered a stimulating theory to explain shamanic experience. Unfolded through the five books that have appeared to date, it is too complicated for us to consider in detail, but several aspects may shed light on phenomena that we find archaic people attributing to their medicine men, shamans, and healers.

First, Don Juan, Castaneda's teacher, assaulted the limitations that the ordinary mind imposes on reality. We all keep a world of common sense in place by talking to ourselves interiorly. Don Juan freed this world and removed many of its limitations by exercises that stopped the interior conversation. In archaic societies, where contemplation was more natural and talking less pronounced than in the modern West, stopping interior processes that supported the world of common sense and social convention may have been quite easy.

Second, Yaqui Indians, archaic Australians, and most other

archaic peoples equated the real with the vividly experienced. They did not enjoy, or suffer from, the development of critical reason that the modern West has inherited from classical Greece, Christianity, and modern science. Therefore a dream, a hallucination, or a poetic image could be as "real" as the stone in one's hand.

If we combine these two elements with the power of a strong personality, we find it plausible that a skillful shaman could induce the "perception" of strings by which to travel to Baiame in heaven or acrobatics like those of Don Genaro. Castaneda went on (pp. 262-63) to sketch a "colony" theory of human composition in which there was no constitutive "I." Such a theory eases some of the speculative difficulties that attend the expanding or projecting of the personality in the way shamanic events such as those he described would necessitate. (Though the colony theory runs counter to Western-Aristotelian assumptions, it would be at home in Buddhism, where the central principle is that there is no "self.") One need not ascribe such a sophisticated theory to archaic Australians in order to account for their shamanic flight. Sufficient would be a mythological tradition, current imagination that made such marvels "possible" and socially acceptable, and a labile, impressionable personality willing to entertain them personally.

We have enough psychological studies of the power of suggestion to show that people can "hear" and "see" all sorts of nonordinary things. When there is no control over such perception, we tend to think of mental illness. But controlled suggestion is half the work of all communication, from politics to medicine and religion. In the vivid myth-making world of archaic peoples, controlled suggestion could "real-ize" extensive vistas and scenarios. The quartz crystals placed in the body, the totemic snake with a special message—neither of these violates imaginative possibility. Neither is a nonthinkable, a contradiction, as a square circle is. For the pleasure, vividness, explanation, and other benefits involved,

161

an archaic person could quite reasonably entertain such a shamanic scenario. Working on her needs, her suggestibility, her desire to accredit what tradition and the rest of the group accepted, a strong shaman could well get a sensitive archaic person to "see" the august Baiame and his court.

Case Study: Sacrality in the Feminine Life-Cycle

Recently the study of archaic Australian religion has become the focus of a small feminist protest. Rita Gross, co-editor of a volume on women's religious lives in non-Western cultures, has argued in that volume that menstruation and childbirth functioned for Australian women as religious rituals. Because of androcentrism—bias in favor of men's importance—most scholarship has failed to accord menstruation and childbirth this religious significance. In fact, it has failed to notice that Australian men use women's experience in their own ceremonies as potent metaphors. Let us use this thesis to probe how archaic women, like archaic children and aged persons, participated fully in their people's religious world-view. We shall find that although scholarship has not placed them front and center, women were far from marginal to Australian religious life.

The traditional presentation of Australian ceremonial life stressed men's rituals because they were more accessible to Western observers. However, even traditional scholarship recognized that the exclusion of women from male ceremonies did not mean their segregation from Australian religious culture. "Of course, every child from infancy onward imitates and is taught the behavior patterns which prevail between relations and members of various groups in varying circumstances. In addition, the girl at puberty is taken in hand by women, who prepare her for marriage, teach her some of the myths which females should know, and inculcate in her respect for the ceremonial life of the tribe" (Berndt, 1963, p. 46). True, young males were separated from women when they began the initiation to manhood, and women were kept

162

away from male initiation rites. This practice tempted some observers to desacralize women, but others saw the issue more clearly. "This superficial sex dichotomy, which conceals an underlying unity, has led many writers into the error of assuming that only activity on the men's sacred ground is really sacred and religious, and that, because the executive authority for the performance of such ritual is frequently in the hands of men, women are therefore profane. Assumptions of this kind have clouded the real issues involved in aboriginal religion" (*ibid.*, p. 53).

These quotations, from the article on aborigines in the *Australian Encyclopedia,* appeared in 1963. Mircea Eliade's book on Australian religion, which appeared in 1973, devoted a dozen pages to women's ceremonies, while Isobel White's study of sexual conquest and submission in myths of central Australia, which appeared in 1975, also explored women's roles. It would not be correct, therefore, to read Gross's study as ground-breaking work with no precedent. On the other hand, Gross's feminist consciousness has sharpened her point of attack, making her interpretations more precise.

Gross begins by admitting the extreme sexual differentiation in Australian religious life: women were excluded from men's ceremonies, and men from women's. Also, men's ceremonies were more elaborate, obvious, and time-consuming. Nevertheless, it is wrong to infer from this custom a correlation of masculinity with cleanness and femininity with uncleanness, as some interpreters have, or to infer that women's ceremonies were but pale imitations of men's. Rather, the experiences that women had precisely as women functioned for them as symbols of their adult status as sacred beings. First, women's rituals occurred in secret, signaling their sacredness. Second, they were instituted by the eternal ancestors in the dreamtime, just as men's ceremonies were. Third, their pattern of withdrawal, seclusion, and return to the community was the same as men's. Last, women did not receive fully sacral status until old age, just as men did not.

From these four observations Gross concludes that women's ceremonies were parallel to men's. Australian women were not outside the sacred community; they just participated in the sacred community through different rites.

Although a girl underwent some prepuberty rites, her first major religious time was the menarche. Menstruation was understood to come from the ancestors and so to be sacred. The general ceremonial format was for an old woman to take the girl out of the camp into the bush. There they would make a shade, the old woman would build a fire, and she would perform a smoke-ritual for the girl (to purify her?). The old woman would make the girl sit over a hole in the ground, telling her that she was now a woman. After two months, they would move their camp close to the main group. The girl would be painted and decorated, a sprig of Dahl tree being placed through the septum of her nose. The girl would then walk toward the main camp, carrying smoking twigs. When the women of the tribe saw her coming, they would greet her with songs. The young man to whom the girl had been betrothed would sit with his back to her. She would walk up to him, shake him, and run away, pelted with twigs and sticks by the other women. Then she would return to the old woman in the bush for more instruction. They would gradually move closer to the main camp, and eventually the betrothed couple would sleep on the same side of the fire.

Because few anthropologists have actually observed this initiation, let alone been privy to the teaching that it entailed, its precise significance is unclear. Still, the teaching very likely was a source of pride, inculcating women's self-respect, because at each menstruation until maturity the young girl would have some of her blood rubbed on her shoulders. A menstruating Australian woman was taboo to men, but not impure. Her blood was powerful, magical, sacred; so in all likelihood her initiation taught her the religious import of her new maturity.

The same holds for childbirth. Both pregnancy and childbirth were grounded in myths of the female eternal ancestors, and both marked another degree of sacral status. Childbirth had the fuller ceremonies, which were secret. Children, younger women, and men were prohibited from the place where childbirth occurred. The tribe's old women and mature women who were mothers went apart with the pregnant woman. They danced around her and sang songs to charm her pelvis and genital organs into giving an easy birth. The woman who was to deliver was attended by her own mother and a midwife in secrecy. They would sing more songs to facilitate delivery and prevent hemorrhage. After birth they would cut the umbilical cord, preserve it, and bury the placenta in a secret place. The mother and child would remain secluded from men for five days, and the mother would observe food taboos to safeguard her child. In the interpretation of anthropologist Phyllis Kaberry, the total childbirth ritual was the equivalent of the men's ceremonies of circumcision (Gross, p. 284).

Women's religious experience in menstruation and childbirth also influenced men's ceremonies. Part of the rationale for this influence lay in the ancestral myths. The story of Djanggawul and his sisters, for instance, has the motif that the sisters are perpetually pregnant and giving birth. Djanggawul helps the sisters give birth, an act that suggests that childbirth was not intrinsically taboo to males. The story of the Wawalik sisters adds another facet. The two sisters are traveling. One of them is pregnant and gives birth. When they resume their travels, her afterbirth blood is still flowing. They camp near a sacred well and a python dwelling there is attracted by this blood. The snake makes a great storm as it emerges from the well to devour the sisters. The younger sister keeps the snake away for some time by dancing, but after a while she tires. The older sister cannot dance off the snake because her blood keeps attracting it, and when the younger sister resumes her dancing, she begins to menstruate. The snake finally swallows both sisters. This myth entered the men's ritual, where the snake became a featured player, presumably to symbolize the dangers and powers of female blood.

In addition to such mythic background, the men's ceremonies involved actually mimicking women's experiences. Before circumcision adult men would carry candidate boys the way women carried children. After the operation they would continue the mothering motif. Sometimes the men would even squat over a fire and allow smoke the enter their anuses (a practice of women shortly after they gave birth). The newly circumcised would behave like babies and be taught a new totemic language. At the end of the ceremony the adult males would exhibit the newly circumcised to the community in the same way mothers exhibited their newly born.

The ceremonies of Australian men also mimicked menstruation. Through subincision—the repeated cutting of the underside of the penis—men would obtain large quantities of blood, which they would use in other ceremonies (especially "increase" ceremonies to stimulate growth of game) for bodily decoration. This periodic blood-letting paralleled the menstrual flow of women. In addition, repeated subincision made the penis somewhat resemble the vulva. Groups that did not practice subincision still practiced blood-letting, usually by piercing the upper arm. As one Wawalik informant put it, "That blood we put all over those men is all the same as the blood that came from that old woman's vagina. . . . When a man has got blood on him, he is all the same as those two old women when they had blood" (Gross, p. 228).

Despite their segregation from men's ceremonies, then, the religious experience of Australian women heavily influenced that of men. Birth, and its prerequisite, menstruation, was so lively a metaphor that it dominated all Australian religious life. The progressive entry of the maturing Australian into the realities of the eternal dreamtime was an ongoing rebirth. The most dramatic moment occurred at puberty, but each further step toward final maturity drew on birth symbolism.

Moreover in actual practice older women were not always excluded from men's ceremonies, and men knew enough about women's childbirth rituals to be able to incorporate them into the male ceremonies. The grounding mythology implied that "in the beginning" women participated fully in ritual life, that "in the beginning" men and women were little segregated. The strict differentiation of later times could be interpreted as a fall from the golden beginning.

Isobel White's study of central Australian myths counter-balances this egalitarian interpretation. Essentially the central Australian myths explain customs of later times, when male dominance was well established. Thus they show women fleeing men's advances and appearing to men as threatening. Still, despite the fact that the myths were supposed to be kept secret, as were ritual objects used in men's or women's ceremonies, White found that older women often knew the men's myths and that women ceremonial leaders often were willing to show their secret ritual objects to old men. (Old age frequently blurs sexual boundaries, as though distinctions matter little in fullest maturity.) Later "dominance" therefore did not exclude considerable communication.

Among the Aranda, female ancestors were especially strong. They appeared in Aranda myths as dignified beings with great freedom of action. Indeed, these myths often showed male ancestors cowering before powerful females. Ironically, Aranda men took great pride in these powerful females but condemned their own women (for failure to approximate the heavenly archetype?). Other tribes had myths replete with sexual conquest, in which men "raped" women who pretended aversion or fear. Overall the central myths indicate considerable hostility between the sexes, men envying women their procreative powers and women envying men their social dominance. Still, both sexes found in their rites affirmations of masculinity and femininity, and the richness of the sacral experience of Australian women leaves no doubt that women were integral to the archaic Australian world-view.

Indians, Africans, Australians: Common Themes

Australian, African, and American Indian religions were all very complicated entities. I have simplified each of them drastically to fit the pedagogical needs of an introductory presentation and the spatial limitations of a small book. To evoke at least a little more of each tradition's richness, let us try in this last section to paint existential attitudes that members of these religious traditions, and of other archaic traditions that have continued into recent times, have shared. Perhaps we can best accomplish this by continuing the case-study method.

For the Pueblo and Hopi children whom Robert Coles interviewed, nature was surpassingly beautiful. For the aged Pygmy Moke the forest symbolized divine bounty and provision. For Australian women menstruation and birth expressed a sacred fertility. How well do these convictions cohere with the cosmological myth? I believe they do it quite well. In each of these three cases the natural world overlaps with divinity and sacrality. Without special emphasis on agricultural rhythms or natural forces such as the storm and the rain, more recent archaic peoples have continued the effort of early human beings to harmonize with the cosmos. Similarly they have continued the instinct of early human beings that their fellow creatures, especially their fellow animals, were more like than unlike themselves.

We may strengthen these observations if we verify them in another recent-archaic case, that of a contemporary Eskimo woman. In their recent *Women of Crisis,* Robert and Jane Coles depict the lives of Black, Appalachian, Chicano, and Eskimo women, to show the struggle for independence and the strength and integrity that women sorely tried by circumstance can manifest. As an integral part of each psychobiography that they present, the Coleses discuss the subject's religious concepts, for the self-questioning that the women go through is in each case also a questioning of God.

The Eskimo subject, Lorna, does her questioning in the context of a north Alaskan village caught between tradition and change. Lorna despises what the white invasion of Alaska has done to her people. She hates the snowmobiles and Coca-Colas. Her counter-treasures are the quiet places where she can enjoy the wind and the water, communing with their spirits. With little formality or ceremony, she goes out of herself, much as ancient Eskimo shamans did:

> The Arctic wind takes possession of her, she claims. For brief spells she is no longer herself. She stands still, closes her eyes, . lets her self rise, spread across the tundra, then fade away—the return to her body. She loves leaving, loves coming back. Her eyes see the wind approaching: the aroused waves; the grass ending; the birds tossing, riding their way on the currents, holding to a course. Her eyes contemplate the return of her "spirit": quiet water, a gentle flat land, a new stillness to the air. And always there are the sounds, which her ears crave—the whispers, whistles, strong voices. . . . (Coles, p. 181)

Lorna also felt great kinship with the animals of her land. The ducks and birds and bears seemed to have messages for her. Their simple life under the sun of the short summer was far more appealing than the complicated life the white schoolteachers and ministers were inculcating. The schoolteachers and ministers were always impressing upon her how little she knew. The ducks and birds and bears seemed to say that she knew enough, that appreciating a good day or a peaceful spot was wisdom enough. When the wind spoke to her spirit, she found release from her constrictions and troubles. When her spirit was free to travel, she could meet her friend from Fairbanks, who was available in spirit out on the tundra. Available too were the spirits of her predecessors in the land, the hardy Eskimo women who used to hunt and wander adventurously before modern changes made those activities unseemly. They did not depart the land when they died. They still lingered, still spoke.

One who reads about Lorna shortly after reading about Moke will probably feel they could communicate easily. The strong Eskimo woman and the wise, aged Pygmy both loved their lands fiercely, although one land was mainly ice, the other mainly tropical forest. The Eskimo woman usually wore furs, the Pygmy a breechclout. But each felt nourished, supported, and centered by the land. Each had an umbilical connection, as though the land were "Mother" Earth. Moke was more explicit about the divinity his forest symbolized, but Lorna put such stock in her "spirits" that their two "theologies" would very likely be entirely compatible. The creatures of both their worlds dwelt in a sacred, life-giving whole. For both peace and prosperity lay, not in possessions, not in externals, but in harmony with that sacred whole—harmony felt deep within.

It seems to me that these two informants translate the cosmological myth very attractively. Were we to probe the past histories of their peoples, we surely would find myths and rituals originally intended to inculcate the harmony they now treasure. Because of recent Western influence (or the limited scope of the reports in which they appear) Lorna and Moke are not especially ceremonial. The Pygmies did ceremonialize death, circumcision for boys, and coming of age for girls, but their main religious ritual was the *molimo*. Lorna's people attended a Christian Church, with very uncertain motivation, and she was married in a Christian ceremony. But her own preference would have been to wander among the other species that were "marrying" in the spring, with whom she would have felt more at home. She had nothing like a *molimo*, but she did have an almost desperate desire to commune with spiritual reality. With or without ceremonial, then, these two "archaic" personalities reverenced the divine in close natural form. Their God was near, fruitful, beyond noisy persons, a fullness of power and peace.

To imply that all tribal members were as impressively religious as Lorna and Moke would romanticize archaic religion, yesterday or today. Not only were many archaic lives short, some were brutish. In addition others were riddled with fear and superstition. The village Africans to whom the Pygmies contrasted themselves saw evil spirits everywhere. The Navaho whose witchcraft Kluckhohn studied had a world teeming with malevolence. Ancient Sumer fell well below ancient Egypt in optimism or hope. At times Christians grew obsessive about Satan and witchcraft, Muslims grew repressive toward women and intellectual inquiry. Nonetheless, the archaic mentality usually included salutary symbolizations of the world-immanent God. Usually archaic spirits, gods, saints, and powers offered experiential catharsis and cleansing.

This experiential accent is another of the family resemblances of the archaic traditions. Friedrich Nietzsche, a canny discerner of modernity's ills, insisted on having a God who could dance and sing. The Lornas and Mokes have had such a God, as have their less impressive sisters and brothers. Indeed, for American Indians, Africans, and Australians one usually met God in dancing and singing. The singing rendered the myths—of the Buffalo Maiden who gave the Sioux pipe or the Nummo who formed Dogon culture or the Djanggawul who worked in the Wulamba dreamtime. To remember these paradigmatic events, to draw them again into the present, was to regain "reality." To use their guidance for peace and fertility was to combine reality with salvation—with healing present disorders, obtaining prosperity. Divinity shot through the world of natural phenomena; it was the causality responsible for both bounty and drought. The secondary causalities with which Western sciences deal concerned archaic peoples relatively little. They had some knowledge of astronomy, pharmacology, and botany, but the laws they most assiduously pursued pertained to the great spirit Wakantanka, the sleeping forest, or the local clan god.

C. G. Jung, a pioneer in the symbolism of religious consciousness, has written of his experiences with archaic peoples in Africa and America. Palavers with Africans impressed upon him the importance of darkness and light. The night was fearful to his informants—a domain of sadness. But when dawn ended the night, God arrived. Jung appropriated the experience to his own theory of consciousness:

> At that time I understood that within the soul from its primordial beginnings there has been a desire for light and an irrepressible urge to rise out of the primal darkness. When the great night comes, everything takes on a note of deep dejection, and every soul is seized by an inexpressible longing for light. That is the pent-up feeling that can be detected in the eyes of primitives, and also in the eyes of animals. There is a sadness in animals' eyes, and we never know whether that sadness is bound up with the soul of the animal or is a poignant message which speaks to us out of that still unconscious experience. That sadness also reflects the mood of Africa, the experience of its solitudes. It is a maternal mystery, this primordial darkness. That is why the sun's birth in the morning strikes the natives as so overwhelmingly meaningful. The *moment* in which light comes is God. That moment brings redemption, release. To say that the sun is God is to blur and forget the archetypal experience of that moment. (Jung, p. 269)

The Pueblo Indian Ochwiay Biano gave nuance to this line of interpretation. Jung was sitting with him on the roof, watching the blazing sun rising higher and higher, when Biano pointed to the sun and said, "Is not he who moves there our father? How can anyone say differently? How can there be another god? Nothing can be without the sun." Jung then asked him whether the sun might be a fiery ball shaped by an invisible god. The question seemed to fall outside Biano's pale. His only reply was, "The sun is God. Everyone can see that" (*ibid.*, pp. 250-51).

Whatever the psychodynamics, archaic peoples in America, Africa, Australia and other lands experienced the divinity of the world at vivid times such as sunrise, in vivid places such as traces of the eternal ancestors. Regularly this intercourse with a holy land begot a deepening love. Whether the land was mountainous or level, beside sea or beside desert, it became a beloved. The psychology of archaic consciousness and the sociology of the people were inseparable from the ecology. The Pygmies were the Forest People, as the Ik were the Mountain People. The Eskimos were the people of tundra and ice. As individuals and groups, archaic peoples defined themselves by the battles they had with the mountains or the ice, the gratitude they owed the plains of buffalo, the waters of salmon, the fields of corn. Castaneda's Don Juan generalized this self-definition, making love of the earth paramount to a "warrior's way":

> "Only if one loves this earth with unbending passion can one release one's sadness," Don Juan said. "A warrior is always joyful because his love is unalterable and his beloved, the earth, embraces him and bestows upon him inconceivable gifts. The sadness belongs only to those who hate the very thing that gives shelter to their beings." Don Juan again caressed the ground with tenderness. "This lovely being, which is alive to its last recesses and understands every feeling, soothed me, it cured me of my pains, and finally when I had fully understood my love for it, it taught me freedom." (Castaneda, p. 285)

Bibliography

Baglin, Douglas and Moore, David R. *People of the Dreamtime.* New York: Walker/Weatherhill, 1970.

Berndt, Ronald M. and Berndt, Catherine H. *The First Australians.* Sydney: Ure Smith, 1952.

———. "Aborigines: Religion." in *Australian Encyclopedia,* Vol. I, pp. 45-55, edited by Alec H. Chisholm. Sydney: The Grolier Society, 1963.

———. *The World of the First Australians.* Chicago: University of Chicago Press, 1964.

———, eds. *Aboriginal Man in Australia.* Sydney: Angus and Robertson, 1965.

Berndt, Ronald M., ed. *Australian Aboriginal Anthropology.* Nedlands, Western Australia: University of Western Australia Press, 1970.

Castaneda, Carlos. *Tales of Power.* New York: Simon & Schuster, 1974.

Coles, Robert and Coles, Jane Hallowell. *Women of Crisis*. New York: Delta/Seymour Lawrence, 1978.

Eliade, Mircea. *Australian Religions*. Ithaca, N.Y.: Cornell University Press, 1973.

Gross, Rita M. "Menstruation and Childbirth as Ritual and Religious Experience among Native Australians," in *Unspoken Worlds: Women's Religious Lives in Non-Western Cultures*, edited by Nancy A. Falk and Rita M. Gross. San Francisco: Harper & Row, 1980, pp. 277-92.

Jung, C. G. *Memories, Dreams, Reflections*. New York: Vintage Books, 1963.

Kluckhohn, Clyde. *Navaho Witchcraft*. Boston: Beacon Press, 1967.

Reed, A. W. *An Illustrated Encyclopedia of Aboriginal Life*. Sydney: A. H. and A. W. Reed, 1969.

Sproul, Barbara C. *Primal Myths: Creating the World*. San Francisco: Harper & Row, 1979.

Strehlow, T. G. H. "Religions of Illiterate People: Australia," in *Historia Religionum II*, edited by C. Jouco Bleeker and Geo Widengren. Leiden: E. J. Brill, 1971, pp. 609-28.

White, Isobel M. "Sexual Conquest and Submission in the Myths of Central Australia. In *Australian Aboriginal Mythology*, edited by L. R. Hiatt. Canberra, Australia: Australian Institute of Aboriginal Studies, 1975, pp. 123-42.

Conclusion

Modernity and the Archaic

The counterplayer implicitly present in our discussions of the archaic religious mind has been "modernity." Modernity is scarcely less imprecise than "archaism," but we can fashion a workaday description. Whether one begins modernity with the Renaissance and Reformation or postpones it to the Enlightenment, it implies a change in Western consciousness. Whereas premodern consciousness credited traditional authorities, both religious and secular, modern consciousness stressed individual autonomy. Whereas premodern consciousness found the natural world mysterious, modern consciousness, tutored by rapid success in the physical sciences, found the natural world amenable to mathematical explanation. The common denominator in these and parallel changes was the advance of critical reason. Bruno Snell wrote the pioneer study on the historical origins of critical reason, documenting the shift from *mythos* to *logos* that occurred in classical Greece. *Logos* received a boost from Christian speculative theology, but a bigger one came from Copernicus, Galileo, and Newton. Critical reason has now become the driving force in Western culture, though today it is usually thinned and crabbed because torn from its roots in contemplative experience. (See Voegelin, pp. 58, 316-17.)

The main effect of modernity and critical reason, for our purposes here, was the desacralization of the cosmos.

175

Whether it should have or not (see Jaki), the rise of modern science divested the physical world of divinity. No longer did we explain the world by tales of eternal ancestors, or even by the creation account of Genesis. The modern mind became secular: the world was just the world. It was not the playground of gods, spirits, or venerable fertility. It did not move by rhythms of fearsome night and divine dawn. The world was not even God's raiment, not even the place where God walked and left her vestiges. The world was just the world. It might have problems and puzzles, but it had no mysteries. As best we could tell, the world came from the explosion of a tiny bit of dense matter, and it would run down to cold collapse. Human maturity entailed confronting these truths lucidly, without nostalgia or regret.

So described, modernity is passé. We shall come to the current, postmodern situation momentarily, but we must first underscore the gains modernity worked. Practically, modernity has been responsible for the technology, economics, and politics that separate our world from medieval times. The skyscrapers, international trade, and bills of rights through which we now live and move and have our being all derive from modernity. So too do current medicine, aviation, computers, communications, education, and the like. The better health, food, clothing, and recreation we enjoy are unthinkable without modernity. Unfortunately, so too are our nuclear arms, destructive chemicals, political revolutions, and energy crises. Modernity, then, has been a two-edged sword. The application of critical reason, human autonomy, and secularism has brought many benefits, but also many severe problems. In most current tallies they have taken us to a post-modern consciousness.

In the twentieth century, scientific and political developments have qualified the hegemony of critical reason. As science developed and as analysts took a more careful look at what scientists actually did, the rather mechanical understanding of physical science that prevailed throughout the nineteenth century broke down. Relativity physics and quantum mechanics found more mystery in the cosmos than Newtonian physics had suspected. Epistemology (the study of human knowledge) after Hume and Kant found it had to give more weight to intuition, myth, and common sense, as well as to the grounding spirit in which critical reason lay. Political science came to realize that both Marxism and capitalism were seriously flawed. Economics came to realize that the new international order was escalating the conflict between rich nations and poor. As the seas, the skies, and the land all became polluted, technology came under attack. As racism and sexism became clarified, their ties with white, male critical reason made its "objectivity" noxious. Depth psychology showed how self-serving "objectivity" could be. The analysis of class-conflicts made plausible the concept that every "objective" truth is partially the product of some group's vested interest.

The upshot was a death-blow to the self-confidence modernity had nourished. On every side were massive signs that we had opened Pandora's box. The experience of two world wars put an end to modernity's pretensions to wisdom. From the Nazi concentration camps to the mushroom cloud of Hiroshima, the vaunted expertise of those reared on critical reason lay discredited. In pursuing our new knowledges and new powers, we had run aground on the old vice of *hubris*. But whereas *hubris* in classical Greek tragedy brought only a limited downfall, our overweening pride threatened the entire creation. Where did we go wrong? What false steps began this fatal sidetracking? Since World War II, a great deal of intellectual energy has gone into answering those questions. And although nothing like a complete consensus has emerged, one can see definite lines of convergence. The riveting pattern for our purposes here is the revival of archaic features that so many of the "answers" postulate.

To be sure, one must understand this "revival" correctly. There is little call for us to return to the forest, and no call for us to return to high infant mortality or widespread superstition. The revival most critics implicitly postulate is really an advance. It would fill out critical reason—balance and complement its great powers—by renewing a veneration of nature, a regular exercise of story and ceremony, an appreciation of "feminine" intuition and reverence for life. More or less knowingly, more or less shrewdly, much of the postmodern critique of modernity has been asking for a repristination of religion, to put Humpty Dumpty back together again. Set in mutual critique and mutual helpfulness, science and religion might become a mandala—a symbol and form for a human whole.

The mutual critique has many levels and aspects, but its core is simple. Religion asks science to limit itself to its proper province and not be scientism. The empirical investigation and logical analysis that drive science are immensely valuable, but limited. When they pretend to obviate the need for holistic contemplation that relates the human person to reality as a unity or the need for politico-ethical analysis that sets science and technology in the service of the common good, these constituents of science become vicious, disordered, destructive. On the other hand, science asks religion to repudiate its past obscurantism. In the past, religion too has overstepped its competency, producing such vicious, disordered, destructive phenomena as the Galileo controversy and the Inquisition. The church overstepped itself then, pretending that theology could substitute for science or humane political theory. Today the church should know better, as science should.

Practically, the revival of archaic virtues that would be an advance to the postmodern consciousness we need takes aim at all four poles of reality: nature, society, the self, and divinity. To a world in ecological crisis the archaic religious mind obviously speaks volumes. We may not be able to bow to the sun, but we had better rapidly shift our energy programs to the sun's power. The sea may not immediately intimate the eternal feminine, but unless we treat both the sea and the land a fragile mother, we shall have no good life. Sociologically we continue to suffer great problems of scale. Our social and political units are too large for us to know one another in the ways that make community, yet we also refuse to comprise one world and make one species. Archaic life could teach us a great deal about forming a people from simplicity and sharing. It could direct modern communications to the realistic goals that world community entails. Food, shelter, and shared meaning were enough for the first 99 percent of human time. Were we free and wise to the measure of some of our simple forebears, they might revive communal joy today.

The self today is fragmented and protean—barely able to contain the horrors it has seen. The detritus of modernity has left the self uncontemplative, ignorant of its primordial vocation to embrace the real. Archaic shamans and yogins remind us that the self has deep hungers it must feed. It wants to commune, make sense, rest at a still point. In a word, the self wants to pray. Any contemporary who does not know what that means is a sad victim of modernity. The same holds for any contemporary who does not know the nonidolatrous import of "God." God is the mystery inseparable from being human. God is the reality, the sacrality, that our deepest moments probe. The beginning and beyond we never grasp are God the definer, the constitutor, of all our selves. Archaic peoples knew this indisputably. Their every sunrise tokened a life-giving parent. Can anyone deny that Moke's forest or Lorna's spirits entail the deepest human significance? I think no one can deny that wisely, in fidelity to the way humans really live. Really, humans reach after meaning and assume that the whole makes sense. Disciplined dialogue between the archaic and the modern could advance our humanity a quantum leap.

The Oldest God

Since society and the self preoccupy most analysts, I shall prescribe for their domains only indirectly. Nature and God focus especially promising trends in current religious thought, so they will be my direct foci. Because ecological and feminist issues stand out in this especially promising religious thought, I shall underscore their pregnant archaism.

Today the horrors of ecological devastation are widely bruited. One need only mention Love Canal to portend a horrible future. Love Canal epitomizes not only a deep disregard of human welfare but an even deeper disregard of nature's integrity. The disregard of human welfare allowed the Hooker Chemical Company to disperse chemicals that ate into children's genes. The deeper disregard of nature's integrity allowed both Hooker and most commentators to discuss the affair with no mention of nature's rights. Recently ecologists have begun to agitate for giving nature rights in law. Their argument is that only when statutes guarantee some safety to wildlife, waters, and grasslands will blind Americans respect them. The argument may be contested at points, but its main drift is incontestable. We latter-day Americans are not like our predecessors in this land. Few of us scruple to rip the bosom of our mother the earth, because few of us feel any religious reverence for her.

The roots of this attitude, and its precise part in the ecological crisis, are complex issues on which there is no firm consensus. Lynn White, Jr., attributed Western brutality toward the land to biblical religion, arguing that biblical religion set human beings free to subdue the earth. Placing God outside the world and making Adam and Eve the head of creation, biblical religion desacralized the cosmos. Biblical scholars have attacked White's interpretation, saying that it seriously misreads scripture. Nonetheless, it seems fair to say that, overall, Western peoples did combine their exalted views of God and human dignity to downgrade the worth

180

of the land. The land was "for" human beings, placed there by God for their good pleasure. It had no independent status, let alone a primacy of dignity. For all that Eastern peoples often abused their lands, deforesting and eroding them, their cultures gave nature more status. The Tao that undergirded Chinese nature stood against deforestation. The Buddha-nature that was simple and uncomplicated shone more brightly through natural phenomena than through complicated, divided humans.

The equivalent was true for archaic peoples, as our previous chapters have suggested. Ernest Callenbach is on the mark, then, when he fills his *Ecotopia* with archaic features. People who love trees, reverence their crops, prize clean water and air—these people avoid ecological disasters. They sense that life, or even simply matter, has a dignity and an integrity that call for respect. Something is untoward in the person who abuses nature, tearing it apart without a care, just as something is untoward in the person who abuses women, children or people of another race. Like nature, those abused people often are relatively helpless. Their claim on us for fair dealing is more moral than physical. The test of our worth is what we do in such situations, as the test of our foreign policy is how we treat nations we could easily bully.

In archaic times, to be sure, nature was more formidable: much of archaic respect for nature was born in fear. But beyond fear were wonder and gratitude. Nature still offers many warrants for wonder. Annie Dillard has reported that a single plant of winter rye sent forth 378 miles of roots and more than 14 billion root hairs. The length of the root hairs in a single cubic inch of soil totaled 6,000 miles (Dillard, p. 164). Is that not wonder-ful, prodigious? Should we not render applause? And should we not still be grateful for the light of our eyes and the air we breathe, the food we eat and the water we drink? If we cannot feel wonder and gratitude with the mythical fullness our ancestors felt, we can at least muster a little common sense. E. F. Schumacher has written about economics as if people mattered, and about truly good work. In both cases he has stressed simplicity, conservation, going with nature's processes. By simple calculations on the back of an envelope, he has shown the folly of basing our economy on irreplaceable fossil fuels. From years with the British Soil Association, he has mustered irrefutable statistics that maximum agricultural efficiency comes only when people farm small-scale, with tender loving care. One can be tough-minded about these matters, or tenderly intuitive. The upshot is the same: statistics and humane intuition both agree that our small planet only has a future if we foreswear our foolish ways.

We are not likely to change our destructive life-style, however, unless we are converted to nature's sacrality. Christian theologians could so convert us, were they to put their imaginations to a new Christian sacramentalism. Following John the Evangelist and John of the Cross, Francis of Assisi and Benedict of Nursia, they could make the world instinct with God's Spirit. But theologians have yet to get their imaginations in gear, and so radical feminism has taken over the ecological play. The good witches whom radical feminist religion solicits would return the spotlight to Mother Earth. Their religion emphasizes fertility, cyclicism, ceremony, and celebration. It stands on the side of life, stands against dichotomies that kill. The dichotomies of mind and emotion, nature and humanity, man and woman, myth and analysis, have all contributed to our currently lethal culture. Over-throwing patriarchal religion (which they do not always understand), the new witches venerate the moon and the stars, the flesh and the womb. The spiral dance that Starhawk advocates will not suit all feminists, but few who appreciate archaic religion will fail to see its beauty.

The correlation between women and nature has a long history, so much in the conjunction of ecology and feminism has great precedent. Exploring another dimension of this correlation, Dorothy Dinnerstein has had recourse to mythic symbolism to focus the beastiality that our current sexual arrangements produce. By the ways we rear our children and align the sexes, we have been producing mermaids and minotaurs—destructive creatures only half human. Dinnerstein seems ambiguous about religion, but she does place it with art and sexual play as a resource for overcoming human dividedness—a resource for reversing the lethal social and ecological routes along which we now career. Women's literature seconds this judgment. (See Christ.) Doris Lessing, Margaret Atwood, and Adrienne Rich, to name just three, all want to dive beneath the wreck of current deculturation and salvage human life. Putting away stereotypically masculine ways of nonrelating to nature or other people, they want a culture that would nurture, make ties, go gently rather than brutally. Their imagery and intent are reminiscent of nothing so much as Taoism, whose *wu-wei,* creative not-pushing, is nature's way. Taoism came from the depths of archaic China, where nature was a divine field. Consciously or not, current feminist religion is the curl of a wave to resymbolize the divine field and escape Armageddon.

The oldest God is nature—that should be clear by now. In the beginning, human beings sensed that their habitat was sacred. With twists and turns and numberless permutations, they played out this primal intuition. Like children with a kaleidoscope, they made the component pieces fall into different combinations. But always the depths or roots or ground of their here-and-now life was sacred—"really-real" and valuable, as opposed to untrustworthy and passing. The message archaic religion brings us in these last years of the twentieth century is but an application of this oldest theology. Our task is to find a way to make the world venerable, lovable, again. We could do this by retaining the transcendent God of the Western world religions, or by accepting Eastern theologies. We could try to dance like original Americans, or fashion new fertility festivals.

But the concrete means are less important than the inspiring

183

intuition. If we revive the sense that God, the ultimate treasure, is instinct in our social and natural lives, we shall catalyze the energy needed to keep history from derailing fatally. If we do not revive this sense and do not develop people who love the earth, history will end quite soon. The old two ways, of death and life, are especially clear right now. Archaic relgion tells us to choose life. It says the oldest God could make all things new.

Bibliography

Brown, Michael H. "Love Canal and the Poisoning of America." *The Atlantic Monthly*, 244/6 (December, 1979), 33-47.

Callenbach, Ernest. *Ecotopia.* New York: Bantam, 1975.

Cassirer, Ernest. *The Philosophy of Symbolic Forms, 2: Mythical Thought.* New Haven, Conn. Yale University Press, 1955.

Chadwick, Owen. *The Secularization of the European Mind in the Nineteenth Century.* Cambridge, England: Cambridge University Press, 1975.

Christ, Carol P. *Diving Deep and Surfacing.* Boston: Beacon Press, 1980.

Dillard, Annie. *Pilgrim at Tinker Creek.* New York: Harper's Magazine Press, 1974.

Dinnerstein, Dorothy. *The Mermaid and the Minotaur.* New York: Harper & Row, 1976.

Jaki, Stanley L. *The Road of Science and the Ways to God.* Chicago: University of Chicago Press, 1978.

La Fleur, William R. "Saigo and the Buddhist Value of Nature." *History of Religions,* 13/2 (November, 1973), 93-128, 13/3 (February, 1974), 227-48.

Schilling, Harold K. *The New Consciousness in Science and Religion.* Philadelphia: United Church Press, 1973.

Schumacher, E. F. *Small Is Beautiful: Economics as If People Mattered.* New York: Harper & Row, 1973.

————.*Good Work.* New York: Harper & Row, 1979.

Snell, Bruno. *The Discovery of Mind.* New York: Harper & Row, 1960.

Starhawk. *The Spiral Dance: A Rebirth of the Ancient Religion of the Great Goddess.* San Francisco: Harper & Row, 1979.

Thomas, Lewis. *The Lives of a Cell.* New York: Viking, 1974.

Voegelin, Eric. *Order and History, IV.* Baton Rouge, La.: Louisiana State University Press, 1974.

Ward, Barbara. *Progress for a Small Planet.* New York: W. W. Norton, 1979.

White, Lynn, Jr. "The Historical Roots of Our Ecological Crisis," in *Ecology and Religion in History,* edited by David Spring and Eileen Spring. New York: Harper & Row, 1974.

Index

Africa, 18, 44, 49, 50, 88, 89, 92, 125-49, 150, 168, 171, 172
afterlife, 24
agriculture, 33-41, 51, 181
Ainu, 26
Akhenaton, 62
Algonquin, 112
Allah, 90, 91, 92, 93, 97
American, 30, 47, 88, 89, 100, 107, 109, 112, 113, 116, 172
American Indians 12, 14, 18, 44, 100-24, 150, 168, 171
ancestor veneration, 42
angels, 84, 87, 90, 91, 97
Angola, 49
Apache, 14, 105
Apollo, 17, 70-72
Aquinas, Thomas, 86
Arabia, 90, 92
Aranda, 154, 155, 156-57, 159, 167
archetypes, 36-41
Aristotle, 73, 74
Arizona, 100
Ashanti, 128-30

Ashvoghosa, 79
Asia, 24, 27, 43, 76
Assiniboine, 117
Aton, 62
Augustine, 86
Australia, 18, 25, 30, 44, 150-74
Austria, 25
Aztec, 47, 100, 111

Balkans, 47, 54
Bantu, 133-34
Basho, 81
beaver, 104
Belgian Congo, 144
birth, 106-8, 164-67, 168
Black Elk, 103
Bodhisattva, 81, 95, 96
Brittany, 46
Buddha, 18, 74, 77-80, 97. See also Gautama
Buddhism, 18, 43, 76, 77-83, 90, 95, 96, 161
Burma, 82-83
Bushman, 132

185

Cagaba, 105
California, 100, 104, 111, 117
Calvin, John, 86
Canaan, 40
Cannibalism, 32, 39
Carnac, 41, 45, 46
Castaneda, Carlos, 159-61, 173
Catal Huyuk, 69
Celts, 88
Cheyenne, 109
China, 22, 28, 34, 48, 50, 54, 74, 76, 80-81, 93, 96, 107, 181, 183
Christianity, 18, 37, 45, 50, 76, 83-90, 95, 96, 161, 171, 175, 182
circumcision, 134, 166, 170
clitoridectomy, 13, 14, 134-35, 156
Colombia, 104, 105
Confucianism, 76, 96
Confucius, 74
consubstantiality, 60-61, 73, 95, 123
Corsica, 45
cosmological myth, 17-18, 72-74, 81, 86, 96, 114, 123, 144, 168, 170
Creator ex nihilo, 83, 104
Crete, 68
Crow, 104, 109
Cupeno, 117

Dahomey, 125
Dakota, 115
Damascus, 93
dead, treatment of, 24-25, 43, 55, 62-64, 112
Delphi, 71

Demeter, 70
demons, 82, 84-85, 87, 88, 93, 97, 157
Dinka, 125, 126, 127, 128, 129, 130, 141
Dionysius, 17, 70-72
diviners, 137-39
Dogon, 130, 133, 134, 135-37, 141, 171
Dumuzi, 58

ecology, 12, 101, 114-19, 121, 151, 178, 180-84
Egypt, 13, 17, 54, 56, 59-68, 72, 74, 92, 93, 171
Eleusinian mysteries, 70
Eliade, Mircea, 79, 87, 113, 163
enlightenment, 81
Eskimos, 26, 29, 47, 107, 112, 116, 168, 169, 170, 173
Estonia, 46
Europe, 25, 30, 32, 40, 42, 45, 49, 50, 54, 87, 88, 89, 153
exorcism, 84, 85

"Fall," 38, 152
fang, 134
farmers. *See* agriculture
Father Sky, 35, 41, 48
fertility, 14, 27-28, 32, 40, 44, 45, 51, 55, 58, 64, 66, 70, 86, 105, 111, 127, 144, 150, 154, 155, 168, 171, 182, 183
Flathead, 104
Four Noble Truths, 78
fox, 105
France, 25, 27, 29, 30

Gautama, 77-80, 90. *See also* Buddha

INDEX

Germany, 25, 88
Ghana, 128-30
God, 52, 73, 83-85, 90, 91, 95, 125-31, 170, 171, 172, 176, 179, 180-81, 182, 183
Goddess, 31, 36-41, 45, 56, 68, 69, 70. *See also* Great Goddess, Great Mother, Mother Earth, Mother Goddess
Great Goddess, 16, 43, 44, 47. *See also* Goddess, Great Mother, Mother Earth, Mother Goddess
Great Mother, 27, 40. *See also* Goddess, Great Goddess, Mother Earth, Mother Goddess
Great Spirit, 103, 104, 106
Greece, 17, 50, 68-74, 88, 161, 175
Greenland, 47
Guatemala, 88
gypsies, 49

Hainuwele, 35-38, 65
Haiti, 88, 89
high god, 103
Hinduism, 69, 76, 79, 82
Homer, 68
Hopi, 46, 112, 120, 122, 168
Horus, 61-65
Hottentots, 132
hunters, 22-31, 56, 104, 153
Hypogeum, 45

Ik, 131, 144-45, 173
Inanna, 58
Inca, 47, 100
India, 30, 34, 43, 48, 50, 54, 56, 68, 74, 76, 77, 79, 82
Indonesia, 35, 36, 38, 46, 65, 76, 94
initiation, 133-37, 151, 156-59
"intermediate plane," 78
Iran, 55, 68
Iraq, 55, 56
Ireland, 46, 87
Iroquois, 110, 112
Isaiah, 83
Isis, 64, 65, 66
Islam, 18, 76, 90-97
Israel, 74, 83, 84, 119
Italy, 96

Jainism, 77
Japan, 50, 81, 96, 119
Java, 49
Jericho, 54-55
Jerusalem, 91
Jesus, 18, 37, 83-86, 90, 97
Job, 83
Jordan, 54
Judaism, 76, 83, 84, 90
Kakadu, 154, 155
Kami, 96
Karma, 78
Kimberly, 159
kingship, 57-58, 60-63, 64, 73, 142-44
Kuan-yin, 81, 96
Kurnai, 159
Kyoto, 81

Labrador, 100, 115
Lakota, 106
Lao-tze, 74
law, 59, 91, 153
lenape, 105

187

Lourdes, 85
Lugbara, 140
Luther, Martin, 86
Maat, 61, 62, 63, 67, 73
magic, sympathetic, 23, 29
Mahavira, 74, 77
Mahayana, 81-82
Malta, 44
Mam, 88
Mandan, 118
marriage, 109-10, 153, 170
Mary, Virgin, 87, 96
Mascouten, 104
Mas d'Azil, 32
"master of the animals," 29
Maya, 46, 47, 100
Mecca, 90, 91, 92
medicine man, 156-62
meditation, 77-78
medium, 128
Megaliths, 41-46, 51, 64
Melanesia, 46
memory, 37-38
Menes, King, 59
menstruation, 14, 108, 109, 110, 162, 164, 165-66, 168
Mesopotamia, 56
metal, 40-50, 51
Mexico, 109
Midatsa-Mandans, 110
Middle East, 33, 40, 54
Minoan culture, 68
miracles, 80, 85, 92, 95
Mississippi, 100, 104
modernity, 175-79
Moke, 145-48, 168, 170, 171, 179
Moksha, 78
Molimo 145-48, 170
Montana, 104

Moravia, 25
Morocco, 94
Moses, 83
Mossi, 135
Mother Earth, 12, 17, 35, 40, 41, 44, 48, 49, 51, 52, 66, 69, 104, 105, 108, 115, 170, 182. *See also* Goddess, Great Goddess, Great Mother, Mother Goddess
Mother Goddess, 55, 58, 70, 96. *See also* Goddess, Great Goddess, Great Mother, Mother Earth
Muhammad, 18, 84, 90-93, 95, 97
mystery, 89, 101
mysticism, 130
myth(s), 35-37, 45, 60, 65, 115, 117, 118-19, 125-27, 130, 136, 137, 150-56, 165-66, 167, 182-83

Naskapi, 100, 115
Natchez, 100, 104
Navaho, 11, 12, 15, 107, 108, 112, 171
Ndembu, 137-38
New Mexico, 100
Nietzsche, Friedrich, 171
Nigeria, 125
Nirvana, 78, 82, 96
North Dakota, 118
Nuer, 139-40

Ojibwa, 106
Ontario, 106
Osiris, 17, 61, 63, 64-67, 70, 86

Palestine, 32

Papago, 110-11
Patanjali, 79
Paviotso, 113
Persia, 50, 74
Plato, 68, 73, 74
Poland, 54
possession, 91-92, 127, 128
power, 111
priest, 127, 129, 140-42
prophet, 74, 139-40
Protestantism, 87
puberty, 108, 110, 162, 164, 166
Pueblo, 12, 100, 110, 120, 122,
    168, 172
Pygmies, 14, 144-48, 168, 170,
    171, 173
pyramids, 62-63, 64

Qur'an, 90, 91, 94

Re, 17, 60, 61, 64-67
reincarnation, 34, 112
rituals, 25-29, 105-13, 131, 133-
    37, 150, 157, 162-63, 167
Rome, 50
Rumania, 88
Russia, 54

sacrament, 39
sacred, 121, 151, 162-67, 168,
    176
sacrifice, 39, 44, 102, 131-37
saints, 92-94, 95-97, 171
samsara, 77
Satan, 83, 85, 87, 171
Scandinavia, 50, 88
Sedna, 30
Seth, 61, 64-65, 66
Shahaptin, 105

Shaman(ism), 15, 19, 22, 29-31,
    50, 51, 78, 87, 90, 96, 104,
    113, 114, 116, 156-62, 169,
    179
Shilluk, 142
Shinto, 96, 119
Siberia, 27-28
silence, 134
Sioux, 14, 102, 106, 111, 116, 171
smith, 47-50, 88
Smohalla, 105
Somalia, 91-92
soul-loss, 15
Spain, 25, 29, 32, 41
Stillmoor, 31, 32
Stonehenge, 16, 41, 45, 46
Sudan, 92, 125, 139-40
Sufism, 91, 93, 94
Sumer, 17, 54, 55-59, 68, 72, 171
sun dance, 102-3
supernatural, 103
Swazi, 143
Switzerland, 25, 54

Tantra, 82
Taoism, 76, 96, 181, 183
Thailand, 82
Theraveda, 82-83
Thompson, 115
Thonga, 130
Tibet, 25, 82
Tierra del Fuego, 103
Togo, 125
totem, 26, 29, 151, 156, 161
transcendence, 72
Trois Frères, 30
Turkey, 69

Uganda, 140, 144

Ukraine, 27
Upanishads, 74, 80
Upper Volta, 135

Vajrayana, 81, 82
Venus of Wilendorf, 27
virginity, 109
vision quest, 114
Voegelin, Eric, 17, 72-74, 80, 83
Voudoun, 89

wheel, 57
Wiradjuri, 156, 159
witchcraft, 18, 87, 88, 129, 146,
    171, 182
women, 13-14, 26-29, 40-41, 49,
    55-56, 87, 91-92, 94, 105-10,
    134, 151, 153, 162-67, 168,
    169, 178, 181, 182, 183

writing, 54, 57
Wulamba, 155-56, 171

"X-ray vision," 30
Yahgan, 103, 104
Yakan water cult, 140
Yanomamo, 14-15
Yaqui, 159, 160
Yin, 28
yoga, 43, 79
Yoruba, 125, 126, 128, 130,
    138-39
Yugoslavia, 25

Zambia, 137-38
Zen, 81
Zeus, 69, 70
Zoroaster, 74
Zuni, 112